Darke

VERSE, SATIRE, FLASH FICTION

Annette Corth

Dedication

This volume is dedicated to the memory of Richard Corth, beloved in life, missed in death.

About the author

The author, who resides in senior housing with her elderly cat, has published three books of her writing in as many years. Her other interests include painting, gardening, classical music, theatre, and, most recently, playing pool and mahjongg. For the first time she has included prose as well as poetry in one of her books.

Earlier books by the author

Explosion of Dragons
Turquoise and Mahogany

Some of the pieces in this volume have appeared in other publications.

The cover painting is by the author. The photograph is by Tony Serviente.

The author can be reached at rcorth@twcny.rr.com or at 115 Bella Vista Drive, Ithaca, New York 14850.

Author's Statement

The greater part of my writing is dark in nature, based on recent personal experience and on life in general in today's worrisome world. A lighter side does exist, however, as seen in some of the verse and most of the satire and brief fiction pieces. I have combined prose and poetry in the darker section and in the lighter one, each alphabetically arranged.

Table of Contents

DARKER

LIGHTER

Be a Man!

Pelvis fractured, he lies in his bed of pain,
mind morphine-beclouded, yet screaming
at each minor movement, involuntary
or nurse-generated. *"We must turn you
to avoid clots and pressure sores."*
"You're killing me! Don't touch me!"

Writhing, arms outstretched,
grabbing empty air as though
seeking succor, his ashen, bearded
face and gaunt body ape Jesus
on the cross.

My heart convulses with empathy.
But as I watch, I muse whether women
are indeed braver, can better soldier
through untenable pain.

Beyond Blondness

Why label possessors of dark hair and brown eyes somber, perhaps even evil, whereas goodness is expressed through lightness: fair skin, blue eyes, radiant sunlit blondness? If one starts out blond and gradually morphs into brunette, is he intrinsically good or suspect, a fallen angel or wolf lurking beneath pale wool? Did the Nazis seek to embody godliness in their dream of a fair-haired Aryan nation under their brunet leader?

Why is a blonde woman more likely to be deemed stupid, frivolous, fun-loving, desirable, licentious than a brown-eyed, dark-tressed person? How jarring to watch a peroxide blonde perform a Mid-Eastern dance, cheapening and demeaning it. The sun's jealous wrath victimizes the blond, exacts satisfaction in burning and blistering the skin, the curse of melanoma.

Black-Framed Glasses

Whose companion is this pair of glasses
with its almost rectangular lenses
and delicate black rim and ear pieces?

Why was it abandoned on the extra-long,
polished rosewood conference table?
Who cannot now clearly see the horizon nor
read a terse message on a crumpled pink slip?

Why was a floor-to-ceiling French window
left ajar in the 10th floor executive boardroom?
What is the magnet attracting the crowd
huddled around a shapeless dark object
sprawled on the marble plaza far below?

Blue in a Red Dress

John promised to join her at the country club swimming pool. Perhaps they might rent bathing suits, cool off a bit in the water, splash each other and behave playfully as they had in the recent past.

Bella wore her new red outfit, a long organdy dress with flounced elbow-length sleeves and a wide ruffled skirt. Her matching red hat with its broad brim both enhanced the appearance of her dress and sheltered her light complexion from the intensity of the afternoon sun. She waited near the edge of the pool on a wooden folding chair, leaning her right arm on the back of the empty seat alongside her as though she were embracing someone.

Sounds of laughter and splashing filled the area. People were wading or swimming in the pool or just sunning themselves on the deck. Bella wistfully took notice of several young couples holding hands or engaged in earnest conversation as they faced each other in the water.

Despite the 89-degree temperature, Bella began to experience a chill. Her body tensed as she prodded her memory over and over again to review the last words she and John had had with each other about getting together at the pool. Was it actually for today or had he mentioned another date? She had circled today's box on her calendar with a large red heart and had written John's name inside of it, followed by an oversized exclamation point. Was the appointment for this pool or the one on the other side of town? He did say two o'clock, didn't he?

Perhaps John was in an accident or fell ill and couldn't contact her. Her phone was out of order and she had left the house early that morning. What if he had sent her a last-minute note postponing the meeting and she wasn't home to receive it? Maybe he changed his mind and decided a reconciliation was out of the question. But would he decide to just stand her up, abandoning her to disappointment and humiliation?

Her sense of chill morphed into a feeling of intense heat. She removed the red hat and tried to fan herself into a more comfortable temperature range. She felt that many eyes were on her, wondering why she sat there alone, all dressed up, saving a seat for an invisible companion. Bella was tempted to try to reach John on the phone but hesitated. She didn't want to appear eager, controlling or desperate—traits that had brought about the rift in their relationship.

Then she felt a growing need to go to the bathroom and to find something cold to drink. The need evolved into urgency. Should she dare to desert her post to seek relief? She thought of writing a note to John to tell him she would be right back. But she lacked a pen, paper, and tape to produce such a message and affix it to one of the folding chairs. Anyway, how would John know exactly where she would be waiting for him? She had mentioned to him that she would probably be wearing her white outfit with the green trim. As a last minute surprise for John, she purchased the red dress and hat. He had always liked her in red.

Finally she arose from her chair, strained her eyes once again to look at each man entering the pool area, and then dashed toward the bathroom and fountain facilities. In her haste she tripped on a low step and fell onto the concrete surface of the path to the clubhouse. As she sprawled there, a stream of blood from her broken nose merged with the red of her dress. She awoke in the ambulance on the way to the hospital. She was in pain and was unable to move her left arm and leg. Her dress was ruined from the efforts of the ambulance crew to attend to her injuries.

Twenty minutes after the ambulance pulled away from the country club, a handsome man in his thirties, dressed in white trousers and a blue and white striped shirt, hurried into the club grounds and headed towards the pool. In his right hand he carried a large bouquet of red and white roses and in his left an elaborately-gift-wrapped box. The man squinted as the sunlight reflected off the surface of the pool into his eyes. Then he circled the pool area several times as though he were looking for someone.

Confession

I weep myself dry, eyes burning, gritty.
Sorrow and guilt pour down my face.
My throbbing chest wheezes wild wails.

Forty-five years I never declared: *I love you.*
Now you are ashes in a box, but on clear nights
you hear me and whisper: *I forgive you.*

Dead Zone

The newly deceased roam the dead zone trying
to learn why they have died and what might have been.
They ponder who truly misses them, desperately
wants them back. There is neither rest nor peace
until they know the unknowable, forgive the unforgivable,
forget the unforgettable.

Diamond

You were my diamond,
hard, brilliant, multi-faceted,
whose presence enhanced
beams of moon, light of sun.

Time bared your hidden flaw,
minor, yet significant.
I can now accept and forgive,
but you are irreparably lost.

Carbon to carbon.

A Dozen X Chromosomes

Prudence Anne Patterson longed for a brother, either older or younger, singly born or as twins or triplets. Alas, her father, for some arcane reason, persisted in passing along to her mother's welcoming womb always the same type of companion for her X chromosome. The result? Prudence was the eldest of twelve daughters.

As a new sister appeared each year, the product of precision breeding, Prudence grew more and more unhappy. She wished to be her father's sole princess, but was repeatedly dethroned by Penelope Alma, Petunia Alice, Peggy Aurora, Patricia Alonza, Portia Arlene, Pansy Arugula, Peony Alpha, Philomena Artemis, Patience Angelica, Pacifica Anita, and Petal Anenome. There might have been more babies, but her father's seed supply suddenly petered out. No brothers, none at all.

Life in the Patterson household was surprisingly well-organized. Older girls tended younger girls; clothes were passed along down the family ladder. Not even the older girls had store-bought dresses unless the Salvation Army or local thrift shops were considered sources of new garments.

The profusion of females, all with identical initials, engendered ingenious systems to identify which girl owned what. Finally the parents appended numbers to each daughter's name to help with ready identification. It seemed easier to think of sister number seven or to look for sister number ten rather than to remember their given names.

To assuage her frustration at being engulfed in clouds of female siblings, Prudence escaped into mental games. When the demands of tending her myriad sisters irritated her, she would curse at them in six languages. There was no point in being a natural linguist if you could not put your gift to practical use. "*Verdammter Esel,* take your socks off the toilet tank. *Bruja gorda*, eat your cereal without drooling on the rug." The younger girls lacked the linguistic skill of their eldest sister and laughed at the funny sound of the words that Prudence uttered whenever she admonished the children.

Prudence's skill with languages was counterbalanced by her exotic diet. She never ate food containing seeds— no watermelon, no grapes, no cucumbers nor tomatoes, certainly nothing as gross as peaches or apples or plums or oranges. She had been told at an early age, when inquiring about the facts of life, that babies come when fathers give seeds to mothers. The girl assumed that all the resultant babies, which seemed to come by the dozen, would turn out to be girls. No! No! There was a sufficiency of females in the world, especially in the Patterson household. For years Prudence refused to ingest anything ostensibly seeded, even gagging if forced to try a banana with its barely-perceptible seeds or, ugh, a fig—sticky and full of potential female babies.

When she reached her teen years, Prudence developed an intense interest in watercolor painting. Her parents recognized her talent and encouraged her by providing professional materials and special lessons. She produced many superb paintings, both realistic and surrealistic in style. Her subject matter was executed in vivid colors and always depicted males, animal as well as human, with a pronounced focus on their seed-bearing parts.

Dream

You visit me in hours of endless night
as I with cheeks of salt restlessly seek sleep.

You resemble your old self, the man I loved
and married--benign, smiling, gracious.

The dream, a balm for years growing apart,
atonement for anger, gruffness, lack of trust.

The amorous cat slumbers in your vacant spot.

Drusilla

Drusilla was an only child living on a large estate with her parents, a housekeeper, a governess, and a live-in gardener/handyman. Life was strictly regimented. Everything was done according to a rigid plan, not quite by the numbers but nearly so.

She wasn't bored by her ordered existence because it was all she ever knew. Every week she knew exactly what would be for Tuesday's lunch or Friday's dinner and which day she would wear her blue outfit and which the yellow one. Her school lessons, taught by the governess, held the only element of surprise in her life. She did not have any advance warning of the advent of fractions or the parsing of dependent clauses.

She saw her parents at breakfast and at dinner and was allowed twenty minutes each day of unfettered conversation with them. Otherwise, she could respond to questions but was not expected to start conversing with them outside of the daily twenty-minute sessions. It was permissible to speak with the various servants but not frivolously. Most of her verbal intercourse was with the governess.

On her birthdays she received a modest gift plus a bonus hour of free talk with her parents. Once a month there was a large gathering of family and neighbors. This was the only occasion when she could talk to and play with people her age. Drusilla loved to read and lived her inner life through the books which were carefully selected for her by the governess, with the approval of her parents. She seldom left the family estate except to go to church and, at rare intervals, to go to the few stores chosen by her parents to be fitted for new clothes.

During the summer when she was eleven years old her parents decided to sail to Europe with her to enable the girl to practice her French, Italian, and Spanish and to obtain some firsthand cultural enrichment. The governess accompanied them to look after the girl and prepare her for what she would encounter in Paris, Venice and Barcelona.

Drusilla had half an hour each day to walk around the ship to get her daily exercise and to practice her irregular verbs. She missed her home with its spacious rooms and acres of gardens and woods. Her cabin was small and did not smell good. She frequently became motion sick and had trouble keeping food down. She was forbidden to speak with the other passengers and looked longingly at other girls her age.

On the sixth day out of port the sea became very rough. The wind blew incessantly and the ship rocked up and down all day. Drusilla stood on the deck gazing out at the agitated sea. She felt inundated by a flood of utmost despair. Everything around her seemed dark and sinister. The surging waves became an irresistible source of temptation. As a terrifying scream erupted from her throat and tears cascaded down her face, she quietly slipped overboard into the beckoning waves.

Emerald Urn

Dick, last week your ashes arrived, shipped
via UPS in an unmarked cardboard box.
They were unwanted but, yielding
to familial pressure, I consented
to welcome the cremains of my
aged spouse, whose pelvis-shattered,
emaciated body had been reduced to
a modest pile of powdery gray dust
and a few off-white splinters.

Lacking a container suitable to house
the remnants of the brilliant man
who verbally abused me for 45 years,
I found a tiny antique shop specializing
in boxes, bowls, vases and such.
An adventurous streak of sunlight
found the shop's dusty window
and spotlighted an opaque, lidded
green urn, somewhere between kelly,
turquoise, and malachite, no,
more like the hue of an emerald.
It was marble, dense, lustrous
and could keep a decades-old secret.

The First Seder after Grandpa Died

I, the youngest Rubinstein boy,
found asking the four questions a joy.

At family seders spring after spring,
Grandpa read the Haggadah and would sing.

He taught us how to dip matzoh and why.
Years later the memory still makes me cry.

After we lost him, everything changed,
seder ceremony and rites rearranged.

My little sister, born years after me,
now asks the questions, defines memory.

The Grim Reaper Wears Brown

Weary of his centuries-old robes,
somber black, stifling in summer,
as well as toting heavy, unwieldy scythe,
he transforms his garb into a cloak
of rough-hewn wood, rich mahogany,
close fitting, deeply cowled like
portrayals of the Virgin.

He reveals his hooded face,
shadowed, half-hidden,
a visage benignly stern,
neither skeletal nor terrifying,
confident and compassionate.

I Ponder Twin Mouse Traps

There is room for Mickey and Minnie to die together,
tiny furry paw in tiny paw, daring to discover
who can more swiftly seize the cheese beckoning
in two adjacent, baited death contraptions.

Why are the traps so close together like honeymooners
butting against each other from head to toe? What
kind of cheese is best for fatal entrapment? Should the
cheese be the favorite of the trapper or of the victims?
Is cheddar more effective than blue or boursin? Is there
a correlation between the type of bait and the body
color of the mouse?

Is a wooden or a plastic base on the killer machine more
efficient? And its color? Has anyone experimentally
proven that cheese is more attractive than peanut butter,
either smooth or crunchy?

In the Ice

of your embrace and the chill of your words,
I shudder away the seconds of our final
day together. Vainly I try to thaw
the present, recall those half-forgotten
years, basking in ardor, drowning in joy.

In the Mirror

I see you in our bathroom mirror,
replacing my image with yours.
You are in pain, life-weary,
ready to check out, surrender.

Another glance and you are younger,
hazel eyes clear and twinkling,
with your shy, embarrassed smile
that I always found endearing.

This is the face I want in heart and mind to
remember, not that bequeathed me the fourth of
November.

A Last Poem

81, recently widowed, heart diseased,
stomach refluxing acid, toothless,
legs arthritic, obese, obsessive consumer
of chocolate, unacclaimed watercolorist,
barely-read so-so writer, meager assets
hemorrhaging from Wall Street antics,
eyesight bleary and dimming, dementia knocking
at brain's portal, sharing bed with vomiting
geriatric cat, childless, only support
system moving to distant state, computer
virus-stricken, CD player paralyzed,
microwave convulsing, hands
trembling, she makes a mug of
de-caf tea, puts on a warmer sweater,
shuffles over to decrepit card table,
picks up pencil stub and back of
eviction notice, starts to compose
her last poem.

Lilith

Subtly ravishing, raven haired,
intense azure eyes, slightly Rubenesque,
innocent lips tinged with promise,

Lilith catered to the urgent whims
of Parisian men, providing that which
they never dared ask of their wives.

In 1942, discovering she possessed
a socially-transferable malady, she promptly
joined the French Resistance.

Patriot of the night, Lilith offered gratis
comfort to handsome Nazi officers, put
thirty-four of them out of commission.

Loss

Too often I collapse into tears, sobbing,
baying wolf-like at your death, too long
in coming, too painful to endure.
My brilliant, stubborn, funny, grouchy
mate of 45 years, living your last months
in grueling agony, found release at last.
The pain is now mine to cherish and to keep.
I howl into the void, receive no reply.

Middy Blouses

I always hated those blouses and long black scarves, which made us look like a bunch of pseudo sailors. What we really were was the most incorrigible group at the Hampton State Institution for potentially wayward women. Every day we all wore the same gray blouses and brown skirts, but for formal pictures they made us wear the *Anchors Aweigh* outfits.

Most viewers of the photograph did not realize that the style and shade of what we had on reflected the deportment category we were put into. The white blouses indicated cooperative behavior, positive attitude and presumably virginal status. I will not go into detail about how the last condition was officially ascertained. The light blue blouse represented a transitional status. Only one person was in that category. That's me in the center of the dark middy group, with the dippy hairdo, holding the basketball with HS on it. To us the letters really stood for Holy Shit.

I spent six years at Holy Shit Institution and came out essentially the way I arrived—angry, stubborn, bored, lazy and very insecure. I missed my own mother. She ran away from my overbearing father when I was ten years old. His new wife was an insipid cow who bent to his every wish. No spirit, no ideas of her own, no sense of humor.

I hated the housework tasks assigned to me and got out of most of them by feigning illness or forgetfulness or by doing the chore so badly that my parents gave up trying to get me to cooperate. I could see no purpose in going to school. All I could end up as anyhow was a maid in someone's house or a clerk in an office or a salesgirl in some dumb store. I just wanted to do exciting things and experiment with interesting new ways of experiencing life.

I learned to smoke and to drink and how to please men so they would take me to fun places and give me all sorts of gifts, which I had to hide in my room. Sometimes for kicks I would steal a few dollars from my stepmother's grocery money or take an item or two from stores without paying for them, usually things I didn't want or need. I just liked the thrill of getting away with the shoplifting. I might not have been good academically, but I was very smart at making up stories to cover my various vices, if you can really consider them that.

At 21 I got out of Holy Shit and had to make my way on my own. I got a job as a live-in nursemaid to two little girls, ages 10 and 12. Their mother liked to dress them in sailor blouses. I thought that since they are already in the appropriate uniform, I'd teach them some of my tricks. We now smoke Chesterfields together behind the bushes in the park, and they are quite good at picking up small items at the five and ten. They still don't care for beer, but I'm getting them used to wine laced with honey. They like to sit behind the sofa in the living room and watch me entertain my men friends whenever their parents are out for the evening. I'm slowly teaching them that doing chores around the house is for the birds and that artful lying is the key to success.

Their parents are delighted that the girls seem so happy and are very attached to me. So who's incorrigible?

Mystery of Pain

He claims pain is in the brain
not in a crushed spine,
a burnt face,
a bullet-pierced gut
or his fractured pelvis.

Distract the brain,
console it with morphine,
pretend its pain pretense,
persuade it that agony
purifies, enlightens.

It'll pass. You'll forget,
like a horrific dream,
pumping adrenaline,
immersed in sweat,
crying out in torment,
wishing for death.

No Note

Promotion denied,
job in jeopardy,
chronic cough,
clinically depressed,
spouse estranged,
children on drugs,
cat incontinent,
gambling debt unpaid,
credit cards maxed out,
computer virus-laden,
rent overdue.

Shrugged, ascended to roof,
peered at cars and trucks below,
coughed, wiped away a tear,
tumbled off into space.

No note needed.

No Safe Place

Ultimately there is no safe place.
The world is lousy, irrational,
hostile, lacking a place to hide
or be secure from harm's embrace.

Germs find us, random accidents
hunt us down, forces beyond control
threaten our well-being. Banks fail,
natural disasters occur, wars devour
society, spread anguish, endless pain.

But, hoping for the best, we soldier on.

Now That You Are Dead

Who will rant about how badly I drive our car?

Who will get apprehensive when I want to use your tools?

Who will insist that I learn things your way only and never mine?

Who will bridle at my insistence that I be allowed to write down step-by-step what you are trying to teach me rather than memorize it all?

Who will get agitated if I want to know how to do something before possessing a thorough knowledge of the physics and engineering behind it?

Who will angrily refuse to clear away mounds of shoes, gloves, tools, magazines, and unread mail that pile up around the house?

Who will ask me to find and do things for him but never utter a "please" or "thank you"?

Who will never compliment me on what I do well but freely point out my minutest shortcomings?

Who will play the radio or television at nerve-jarring volume and get grouchy at a request that it be lowered?

Who will bristle at my lack of interest in many of the subjects you enjoy?

Who will resist having anything to do with my family and most of yours?

Who will embarrass me by his scruffy appearance in the name of "comfort"?

Who will belittle and deprecate people who don't go along with your interests and values?

But, who will suffer all of the above, remain loyal and keep loving you?

The Queen

June 1962. Accompanied by her genial older brother, the little girl posed in front of the porched house in her Sunday best. But her fists were clenched, her lower lip protruded, and her feet were set in a stance of intractable defiance. Who was this hellion? What was she objecting to? Her brother, in the speckled light, presented an image of guileless serenity.

Little Angelica did not want to attend the christening ceremony for her new sister. One girl in the family was all that seemed necessary or desirable. It was bad enough that she had to compete with her brother for parental attention and favors. "But he's older. He's a boy. Girls don't climb trees. Girls can't be taken to chicken hatcheries or dude ranches." Angelica was much smarter than her placid sibling and reveled in her excellent grades and superior musical ability. Somehow she could cope with the one-on-one rivalry, but to have a third child in the family appeared unbearable. Her grandparents and aunts and uncles always fussed over her, the only girl in her generation. They hugged and kissed her, exclaimed over the beauty of her golden hair, and took pride in her perfect pitch. She loved being the adored queen. It almost made up for the lack of privileges that her untalented brother enjoyed.

Throughout her mother's third pregnancy Angelica acted up. Her displeasure at the coming of the intruder grew in direct proportion to the size of her mother's ever-expanding belly. The girl feigned headaches and upset stomachs.

She "accidentally" dropped dishes she was supposed to dry. Her robust thrashing about in the bathtub created many floods that would escape under the bathroom door. Her brother's homework papers often got misplaced or had errors forged onto them. She stopped letting her mother hug her good night. Angelica prayed that the new baby would become sick and die.

The christening day arrived bright and warm. Angelica was cajoled, actually bribed, to put on her new red outfit and pose for a picture with her brother before going to the church. In her head she reiterated a mantra: "I hate that baby. I hope she dies. I hate that baby. I hope she dies." During the christening ceremony she loudly pretended to cough and sneeze. She moaned audibly that her head hurt and she was going to be sick. The baby's sudden shrieks and fit of vomiting preempted her complaints. The ceremony abruptly halted and the frantic parents rushed the ailing infant to the emergency room. Convulsions ensued while the medical staff fought to stabilize her.

Angelica and her brother were in the hospital waiting room with their grandparents when the word came that the baby would be all right but may have suffered some degree of brain damage, not apparent at the moment, but possible to manifest itself in the future. The older girl swelled with pride. She had cursed her infant sister and now had concrete evidence of her own great power. The new upstart would never be able to compete with her. The queen had retained her throne.

Reunion, No

I don't want a reunion with them. I want revenge. I want closure, the last word, a chance to state my case, express my feelings, maybe verbally blacken some eyes and bloody a nose or two. I didn't acknowledge until now that aspects of many relationships and events in my life were still festering, engendering anger and frustration at missed opportunities to stand up to people and to plead my case or explain my feelings.

One person I want to encounter again is a then-13-year-old schoolmate, Barney Boardman, a handsome, arrogant bully, the son of a local gangster. In one of our grade school classes he was selected to choose boys and girls to be on his team. Another boy suggested my name. With a sneer, Barney dismissed the choice with the statement: "She's illiterate." Sixty years later the pain and sense of outrage at the insult remain. I can still visualize the scene. I want to confront Barney Boardman, even if he is still in prison, and respond to his evaluation of me. Illiterate? I was an A student and a voracious reader. I now have a master's degree and am a published poet. I am no longer too shy to defend myself. OK, Barney, shove this between your bars!

Then there is Wilma Lindsley, the library school professor who taught the advanced reference course I took while earning my MLS. I loved that class and did A work in it. Miss Lindsley was a dour spinster who favored the few males in our class, but she was an excellent instructor. A few years later as I was interviewed for a new library position, I was informed, off the cuff, by a potential employer that I should not use Professor Lindsley again as a reference. I still don't know why she gave me a negative recommendation as a reference librarian, but I would love to face her and demand to know what she had said and why. I think she has passed on to the great library in the sky, but I am still eager to grill her, even via special e-mail.

Additionally there was Greg Lunderman, the suave bastard who led me to believe he was unmarried. True, I was blind to clues about his duplicity, but wanted to trust him when he said outright that he was single. I was so gullible. His job took him overseas for a few weeks and he sent me cards from France and from Germany. I longed for his return. One afternoon I was on my way to a museum in Manhattan when I spied him, walking hand in hand with a short woman, wearing a huge diamond ring, and holding the hand of a young girl. I ran up to him and said: "I thought you were in Europe." He didn't miss a beat, but pretended that he wasn't sure of my name or who I was. Then he introduced his wife, and the Lunderman family strode away. I was shocked, flabbergasted, devastated, paralyzed. I wanted to cry out that we had been seeing each other for months on more than a handholding basis, but I hesitated. I didn't want to upset the child and his wife. Now I regret my compassion. I want to tear into him for his betrayal of both of us. For years I fantasized about being behind him in a subway station and shoving him in front of an oncoming train. Indeed, hell hath no fury like a humiliated woman.

Rite of Writing Right

When writing about writing, I ponder
syntax, rhythm, metaphor. Dusty prisons
delineate the size, shape, pattern
of my words and emotions, which beat
in tears against bars of rust. Words try
frantically to create themselves, be feral,
soar or swim, race or weep at will.
Constant struggle with rules and tradition,
caveats and requirements hemorrhages
my muse, stifles my spirit.
I write on.

Secondhand Menace

His hat warned me. Its shadow on the wall in the front entrance and its presence on his head, pulled down low over his eyes, jumpstarted my panic reflex. It was just a hat, a handsome medium-size, black Stetson with a high crown and broad brim, held in place, cowboy-like, with a long leather thong. But this secondhand object terrified me.

I purchased the hat at a Salvation Army store and as a half-joke presented it to Victor on his 30th birthday. To my surprise and satisfaction, he immediately fell in love with it and spent a long time in front of the hall mirror admiring how it looked tipped forward or to the side or straight on, brim down low over his face.

Gradually I became aware of slight changes in Victor's behavior, especially when wearing the hat. His eyes narrowed and grew darker, he began to swagger about the house, his voice morphed from a gentle tenor to a raspy, grunting baritone. He lost patience dealing with the children and resented my asking him to help around the house. He began wearing the hat constantly both indoors and out as though it were a sign of religious piety. It was the last thing he removed before getting into bed.

Victor began criticizing my housekeeping and child care, complained that I couldn't manage money well enough anymore, and grew angry if I went out with my friends or to a meeting without his permission. He no longer discussed anything with me beyond immediate domestic matters. Dissent was not tolerated as he assumed the role of marital despot. Our sex life became brutal and one-sided. My needs were not only subservient to his, but gradually became totally ignored.

I managed to prevent him from physically disciplining the children but suffered his wrath personally on many occasions with resultant welts and bruises. He struck me only in places on my body that are covered by my clothing. No one saw any evidence of his abuse.

Things escalated when he started wearing boots instead of regular shoes. I tried to speak to him about the changes I saw in his once loving demeanor, but he refused to take part in the conversation. A punch to my rib cage ended all attempts to communicate with him. Victor lost his temper when he learned I had tried to seek help from my family and from our minister. The children began to have nightmares, lose their appetites, and do poorly in school. Victor blamed it on my shortcoming as a mother.

I had no money of my own. Where could I go with three young children? Would he really track me down and "beat the living shit out of all of us" if I attempted to take the children and leave him? I cursed the day I ever bought him that Stetson from hell. Maybe I could take it away when he was asleep or in the shower and throw it out or, better still, burn it. Risky, but I was desperate. Either he would revert to his former self, the gentle caring man I married, or his rage would destroy all of us.

I wondered who had owned the hat before it landed in the Salvation Army store. Did it wreak a similar metamorphosis in him?

One night I quietly arose from our bed, made certain that Victor was snoring away, and snatched the hat. I took it out to the backyard, put it in the trash barrel, added some torn newspapers, and set them on fire. The paper erupted into flame and surrounded the evil sombrero with smoke.

Behind me I heard the back screen door open and slam shut. Victor, naked, was running toward me waving his arms about and shouting. In one hand he carried a large jar of bottled water and in the other his hunting knife. Its blade gleamed with malevolence. I began screaming, "No! No! Please don't!" Our neighbor heard the commotion and emerged from his house, flashlight and shotgun in hand. The situation resolved itself with suddenness and with blood. No trace of the hat remained in the trash barrel.

Song of India

I have never visited India, my impressions of that teeming, other-worldly sub-continent derived from motion pictures and television. Hectic scenes of unimaginable overpopulation and nightmarish poverty accompany my virtual experience of the odors, smells, scents, fragrances, and olfactory insults emanating from perspiring bodies, alien cooking, burning corpses and reeking river pollution.

In a catalog offering attire for upscale American females, I find an ad that makes me reel, *"Song of India" hand-carved soapstone jars containing purest perfume solids.* I imagine the reek of garbage, decaying fecal matter, and over-seasoned curry. The three kinds of perfume in the catalog claim to be sandalwood, patchouli, and Krishna Musk, at $14.95 each, two or more for $12.95. I decide to pass.

Tarot Image

Emperor Joukahainen, regally attired, enthroned,
glares at the world, grim-faced, brow-furrowed,
mouth ascowl above long tapering gray beard.
His mountain realm, drab and forbidding,
reveals few signs of verdure, the only visible green
the orb defiantly grasped in his left hand.
The subjects of this empire, delicate, slender-faced
sheep with inwardly-curved horns, the only mammals
capable of surviving so far above sea level.
The lone human, ruler of thousands of bovines,
fruitlessly awaits a mate.

Three Sounds

She sits on the seat in her bathroom
overlooking the stormy shore below,
sadly listening to pebbles crash
as agitated waves carry them
in and out. She desperately awaits
a call from an estranged lover,
but first answers the call of nature.

Jittery, heart rate accelerating,
she opts to be assertive,
punches out the numbers of his
cell phone on hers. No answer,
just the beep that beckons voice mail.

Sobbing, she wipes her moist eyes
with the hand holding the phone,
loosening her grip. As she rotely
pushes the flush button, the free-falling
phone spirals down the bowl.

To Tell the Truth, Not

I loved to torment my three younger brothers, Jeremy, who always wanted to be a ballerina, and the twins, Jim, who ate dirt, and Kim, who liked to pee on ants. Our mother utilized a different casual date to create each of us and gave me the onerous responsibility of being an ad hoc guardian of her whelps while she cruised around looking for sperm from more exotic men. She had had it with Caucasians and was now actively pursuing Chinese, Japanese, Korean and Thai men. So far she was unsuccessful in persuading any of them to help her produce more colorful offspring.

I told Mom that I was helping Jeremy select Halloween costumes when I lent him my padded bra and a short full skirt to wear in the park. He thought that the jeers of his peers were merely expressions of envy at his grace and beauty while he pirouetted around the baseball diamond and did a slow plié as he rounded each base. I encouraged his weird behavior.

Jim and Kim were unwelcome additions to our family. One brother was enough even though I was trying to turn him into a pseudo girl. Mom was not only a bit ditsy in social matters, but she was also clean crazy. Hands had to be washed at least six times a day, certainly before and after each meal. The same applied to the brushing of our teeth. Fruit and vegetables were soaked and vigorously scrubbed before cooking. We were forbidden to eat them raw—too full of pernicious germs out to poison innocent humans.

45

I took Jim aside at any early age and showed him how to make candy out of dust puffballs and crunchy treats out of cat litter. A little cinnamon and a bit of peanut butter and he felt he was ingesting ambrosia. I did caution him to rinse out his mouth before Mom checked up on his general sanitation.

Kim, on the other hand, disdained my gritty concoctions but was enamored of my suggestion that he would grow up to be a Marine sharpshooter if he practiced peeing on ants whenever he saw them or felt the need to diminish his store of liquid ammunition. His teachers were somewhat unsympathetic towards his practicing this skill in the classroom so he confined his shooting to outdoors. I must admit that his accuracy at forty-five inches was amazing. He took to drinking water and soda in excess to keep his weapon fully loaded. What a buzz it gave me to have friends and family comment on my good deportment as they deplored the aberrant behavior of that bunch of male losers.

Wall Hanging

Quilted pot holder, too beautiful to embrace
objects too hot to handle. Semi-abstract
geometric patterns, cool hues of greens
and purples randomly kissed by pink.
Perfection too sacred to touch, enshrined
on altar of awe, bereft of purpose.

Where Are You?

I want to tell you what I did today.
Where are you? Come home.

What do you think about my new poems?
Where are you? Come home.

I need help again with the computer.
Where are you? Come home.

The dishes in the sink are piling up.
Where are you? Come home.

We are late for lunch with Nancy and Harry.
Where are you? Come home.

Dakota called about playing chess tomorrow.
Where are you? Come home.

Our new car is making strange sounds again.
Where are you? Come home.

Be sure to use your walker. I don't want you to fall.
Where are you? Come home.

You fell and shattered your frail old body.
I know where you are. You will never come home.

White Flame

Flickering and wavering, a white flame
yearns to know whether its lack of color
indicates extreme heat or extraordinary cold.

Atop a rustic pulpit, ash from a burning
scarecrow sparkles like moonlit crystal
or the halo of ascendant saints.

A jagged tear in the flaming straw figure
exudes the scent of alien spice, simultaneously
bitter, pungent, overwhelmingly floral.

In answer to its cry for mercy, a small
azure bird swoops downward to the pyre,
dousing the flame with golden tears.

Chocolate

Succulent brown goddess,
creator of joy and passion,
balm for the bereaved,
beloved of tongue and nose,
prized among all gifts,
I worship you, praise you,
lust after you, would die for you.

The Curse of the Purse

My purse reflects my soul and protects my body. It is the equivalent of carrying mace or a blackjack. True, its dense mass has altered my posture inasmuch as my right side tilts downward and the shadow of a ridge sits on my bare shoulder. The purse itself is bereft of even a cubic centimeter of unused internal space.

I purchased this pocketbook (which is neither a pocket nor a book) because I needed a replacement for its exhausted, well-worn predecessor. As usual, I selected the largest bag I could find that had a single, long shoulder strap. I was delighted to find one that appeared to meet all of my criteria regarding size, strap length, multitude of internal separators, and zippered compartments. Also it was black.

Please note the verb "appeared" in the previous paragraph. When I arrived home with my new acquisition, I surrendered to the pleasure of unstuffing it (why do they puff them up with all that wadded paper?) and situating the contents of my moribund bag in their new home. I removed and discarded the flock of tags enumerating country of origin, designer name, content of the material used in its manufacture, propaganda expounding the beauty and utility of the object I had so wisely acquired, the identifying bar code, the price, and the number of the worker who had inspected the bag.

The purse was now ready for its debut as part of my persona. At that point the first evidence of the curse manifested itself. The bag was not black but navy blue! The mismatch offended me as an artist since black, neutral and basic, is at the heart of my wardrobe. I felt that all eyes would rest on me when I went out in public, clucking figuratively at my black shoes and socks, gray slacks, black sweater, and green coat embellished by, ugh, a navy blue purse. Since I had unambiguously established my ownership of the purse, it was impossible to exchange it for one of the proper color. I decided to brazen it out and hope that no one would notice that I always carried the bag on the shoulder in shadow, never on the sunny side of my body.

As I used the pocketbook, the curse struck again. It started to acquire smudges of salt from the car, drips of coffee, smears of unidentifiable dirt. My attempts to remove these scars of my carefree (or is it careless?) existence resist every effort at sanitization, wet or dry. I cringe in chagrin whenever I have to flip open the main flap in front of any witnesses and expose the impurity of my life style. The seeming indifference of store clerks and friends to my streaks and smudges unnerves me. If they would only have the compassion to smile and say something like *Wow, that gray smear really enhances the navy blue of your purse or Hey, I'm a slob too, always dripping coffee or soda on my bag*. This conspiracy of silence tears at my self-image.

The purse, stuffed and ready for action, weighs in between five and ten pounds. It is a cross between a lethal
weapon and a portable convenience store. Annually I
conduct an inventory of its arcane contents but decide
each time everything in it must always accompany me.
Sometimes it is a bit tricky to fit the contents back in
again, and I do tend to forget some of the items tucked
into the lower corners.

My husband mocks me for carrying the pseudo-black
satchel with me at all times. But he does not complain
when I give him affirmative responses to *Do you have an
aspirin, an antacid, a cough drop, a band-aid, a pen, a nail
file, a comb, your penknife, extra car keys, a mirror, paper
clips, an orange marker pen, the checkbook, some paper to
write a note on, the membership card from the video store,
the AAA card, my business cards, some virginal Kleenex, or
a deodorant stick?* To date, he has never asked for my
spare pair of eyeglasses.

My wallet is the chief culprit in adding bulk and weight
to the purse. I do confess that said wallet is crammed
with change and paper money, my eyeglass prescription, family and pet photographs, four different coffee
shop discount cards, outdated health club guest cards, a
multitude of official cards—Medicare, Social Security,
voting registration, driver's license, library card—phar-
maceutical discount card, frequent flier card for a bank-
rupt airline, outdated membership cards from museums
and sundry other organizations.

I cannot discard them. You never know when they might come in handy to clean my nails, shim up an uneven chair or table, or possibly cut up and add to a collage.

Delectable Gold

Apricots, sensuous to eye and tongue,
pervade, suffuse mouth and mind
with sweet/tart perfume of heaven.

Twin trees in our April garden,
decorated with alabaster promise,
miscarry in May's killer frost.

Other years the two trees beget
plump golden fruit, soon ravaged
by insects, birds, rampaging rot.

Delicious Decision

Venerable, string-bearded Confucius lusted in soul and
body
after scrambled eggs, sunny-side-ups, eggs boiled,
poached,
or shirred, omelets both western and foo yung.

But even more the ancient sage savored chicken fingers,
roasted capon, chicken a la king, buffalo wings, chopped
chicken liver, pickled chicken giblets.

Daily at dawn the master ascended the mountain,
faced the emerging sun, and made the same monumental
choice, the outcome of which would affect his destiny
and his revered life, both spiritual and carnal.

"It is better to have a hen tomorrow than an egg today."

Exchange

Gladly would I trade my Star of David,
the mezuzah on my doorpost or your golden
crucifix, flaunting the torment of your god,
or even their beloved Kuran, replete with Allah's
dicta, for a yard-long double necklace
of sumptuous gleaming turquoise shaped
into Egypt's incised scarab beads.

February is for Lovers

True love is its own reward
even if you're very bored.

Matrimony: Precursor to alimony

Dowry: Bribe to accept an unacceptable bride

For better or for worse: Prologue to a curse

A sweet and honeyed word'll
soon begin to curdle.

If fortune smiles, 'twill be your fate
to find an ancient, wealthy, sickly mate.

Since their schedule was so very tight,
she bore her baby on their wedding night.

I love milk chocolate in a box.
My wooer goes for bagels and lox.
First our stomachs we satisfy;
Then the rest of us we gratify.

Electra claims she loves her brother
and often adores her cheating mother,
but lusts after Daddy like no other.

Marital Vow:
To love whether well or sicker,
To whisper sweet words as we bicker,

To stay sober or share our liquor,
And forget our promises to the vicar.

Don't forget
that I, Annette,
am not your pet.
If you deceive me
and try to leave me,
I will kill without regret.

Men call ugly women *Honey*
if their fathers have lots of money.

To woo for cash is quite cruel.
So why not hammer her with your tool.

Handsome men who preen and prance
are often gigolos in France.

One late evening in December
a roué gave a young virgin
Chardonnay and eggs of sturgeon,
promised to love and to honor
as he fell down upon her.
The rest she can barely remember.

The wise mother had a daughter
and diligently taught her
to flirt and tease
and kiss with ease
but not more than she oughter.

The pious and the timid preach
we must each other with love reach,
but when seeking to wed
approach the marital bed
with only one apiece.

First Artichoke

You took me to a multi-starred restaurant,
many levels above my limited experience.

The appetizer you suggested was an artichoke,
a food I had never eaten nor ever heard of.

Diffident and impressionable, I acceded.
Shortly a verdant bulb appeared.

Fork and knife at the ready, I prepared
myself for a new adventure.

You vigorously shook your head, side to side,
at my lack of culinary sophistication.

I was startled to see you, such a suave man,
disdain tools and start to strip one leaf
after another from the green morsel.

You drew each leaf slowly through your front
teeth, relishing the edible matter,
discarding the tough, denuded leaf.

After no unscraped leaf remained, you cut
the pink-yellow pointed top from the inner core
to disclose its gourmet treasure, the heart.

I grew to love both artichokes and you, who
also taught me to appreciate fine wine.

One summer day I met you on Park Avenue,
hand-in-hand with your young daughter
and petite, diamond-bedecked wife.

Food Memories

1. Seeing Red

I clearly remember sitting around the kitchen table sixty years ago with my parents, my brother and my grandfather. We always occupied the same places at the bright yellow table. My father and the father of my mother sat at the head and the foot of the table. My mother and my brother shared the side nearest the stove and the sink, and I had the luxury of having the entire length of the other side just for me. My most vivid food memory of that time was when my mother proudly served bowls of steaming homemade chicken soup garnished with a few lima beans. My father tried a spoonful of the hot broth and promptly showered his bowl with shakes of salt and pepper. He again sampled the no-longer-so-bland soup. (My mother never got into seasoning beyond onion and a bit of garlic.) Wordlessly my father reached for the bottle of ketchup on the table and bloodied the soup with its contents. This finally satisfied him, but my mother was quietly outraged at the desecration of her creation.

2. How Much?

In general we looked upon my mother as a good, certainly more than adequate, cook. She was limited in her repertoire, and we were similarly limited in our knowledge of the vast possibilities of food preparation. I wanted to learn how to cook, to emulate her skill. However, we had great battles, actually angry shouting matches, about exactly how much of what went into a given dish and in which order. It seems that precise measurement was alien to her culinary methodology. "A handful of this or sometimes a pinch of that when you thought it was necessary. Then cook it until it is done." I never did learn to cook under my mother's free-style tutelage. Mom, please forgive me for not recognizing your intuitive skill.

3. Sodium Chloride

The first outburst of anger towards my new husband was generated by a dish of scrambled eggs. I love salt on my food; Dick never touches the stuff. In fact, when he first wrote to his mother about me, he didn't say much about my mind or my body but did declare that I used piles of salt on my food and that I always reached for the salt shaker before I even tasted what was on my plate. One morning he said he would make breakfast and set a lovely mound of loosely-scrambled eggs in front of me. As was my wont, I sprinkled the soft yellow peaks with the saline crystals. I put the first forkful in my salivating mouth and started to scream. To teach me a lesson, my dear spouse had heavily pre-salted the eggs. The addition of my usual amount of salt then rendered them utterly inedible. Suffice it to say, he did not again try to wean me from my beloved sodium chloride. But I do confess that I now sample first and then sprinkle to taste.

4. The Sin

My mother kept a kosher kitchen. We abided by its strictures even though we thought that they were outmoded and needlessly bothersome. During my teen years I belonged to the Civil Air Patrol Cadets and once went on an all-day field trip with the group. It marked my first flight in an airplane, a tail-dragging flivver, and my only experience going through a field of tear gas. But I digress. For lunch we were provided with sandwiches, ham and cheese and butter on white bread. I had never eaten flesh of the pig before nor had I ever been party to a mingling of meat and dairy products. No other food was available. I carefully gazed skyward to see if Jehovah were watching and then bravely bit into the sinful sandwich. I felt very apprehensive about breaking millennia of dietary laws and feared I might get ill or be punished in some other way for my transgression. But, Lord God, how delicious it was!

Fortune Cookie

"Friends long absent are coming back to you,"
regardless of whether you want them to.
If they were friends, they would not stray
but hang around, be there every day.
Sadly enemies, bores, and strident kin
remain at your side through thick and thin.
True friends sometimes must take wing,
but still exist through e-mailing.

Georgia on My Mind

If she were alive today, Georgia O'Keeffe would have e-mailed me to come to stay at the Ghost Ranch. She was very eager to have me as a student in her sole one-person master class. But instead of an electronic invitation—really it was an order—she sent me a terse note stating that it was most imperative that I come there within two weeks and be prepared to remain at the ranch for six months.

I would have my own room and studio space and should bring sufficient art supplies to start me off. And, oh yes, dress was quite casual. Bring stout hiking boots and a warm coat for the cold desert nights. She was familiar with my work, she said, but opined that six months under her tutelage would fine tune it and raise it to a higher plane.

I was ecstatic about receiving the call inasmuch as I loved the intensity of her images and welcomed the challenge of working intimately with this powerful personality. I realized that I would be expected to dress somberly in non-flamboyant colors. Nothing would be allowed to drain the energy of the pigments on the canvas or compete with the austere grandeur of the New Mexico landscape.

I had to bid farewell to my rich and junk-food-laden diet. Simple organic foods were to be the staple of our meals. The closest I would get to meat would be the essence of its former flesh exuded by the various skulls and other bones adorning the sparsely-furnished adobe rooms.

Life there promised to be aesthetic boot camp. Up to welcome the first glimpse of sun and take a brisk 30-minute walk into the scenery, keeping constantly aware of the changing colors and shapes as the light increased with the rising sun. Have a Spartan breakfast in mutual silence, small talk considered a waste of breath.

Then brief instructions about the objectives of the day's work followed by solitary hours at the easel, either in the studio or at selected sites outdoors. She busied herself with her own painting or spent time tending her vegetable garden or grooming her dog.

Precisely at noon I was to present myself at the table for our healthy but bland lunch. Six months of corn and beans and cheese each day. The only seasoning consisted of a few words spoken by my hostess, generally on the subject of the art market or the cost of supplies.

Then came the moment of truth. I showed her what I had painted and she tore into it, verbally of course. *More contrast. Bolder composition. Add a touch of the complement to the shadow. What was the focus of interest?* A priceless critique but soul-withering. A welcome one-hour naptime followed, not voluntary, and then I spent the balance of the afternoon adjusting my work to conform to her teaching.

After dinner, more beans and corn and cheese but with fresh salad and fruit added, probably to ward off scurvy, we discussed—rather Georgia did—the work and promise of other contemporary painters.

Each night I dropped into bed, reeling with mental fatigue and the exhilaration of realizing that my work was gradually being fine tuned. It was still my style but vastly improved by the maestra's tutoring. As I fell asleep each night, I smiled to myself and softly hummed *Georgia on My Mind.*

Grandma's

first name was Shaindl, the beautiful one.
When she arrived here, escaping from
the oppression of life in Russia,
she eagerly Americanized her name,
asked to be known as Jenny.

I do not know how Shaindl
and Jenny are related. Most
Yiddish names are Anglicized
into something similar in sound.
My father, Shmul Yacob, became
Samuel Jacob and my brother,
Hershl Baruch, carried the impressive
name Harris Bernard. He felt Harris
pretentious, perhaps even effeminate,
labeled himself Harry, a name I never liked.
For decades we called him Beanie.
In his seventies Beanie Harris Harry
said he always detested his nickname.

I barely remember Grandma Shaindl
Jenny. She died when I was four.
My only recollection of her
was her smiling presence when my Mom
presented me with my rival, enemy
and eventual friend and benefactor,
Beanie Harris Harry. The newborn
Harris was "skinny like a bean," which
gave him the hated appellation.

Great Golden God

The huge **temple** throbbed with excited murmurs of the faithful as they entered the sanctuary, its vaulted ceiling aglow with azure light. Windowless walls, which insulated the worshippers from the mundane outside world, glittered from an eerie substance, which lent a subtle sense of opulence to the darkened house (more accurately palace) of worship. A large raised platform occupied the entire front of the space to serve as an altar separating anointed ones from the excited masses below. Lush sapphire-blue carpeting covered the entire sloping floor of the main portion of the room. However, the floor of the platform consisted of highly-burnished teak, which reflected the azure light playing on the ceiling far above. A thirty-foot high golden statue dominated the altar region. Its metallic face and rigid stance displayed no discernible emotion.

The sanctuary was spacious enough to contain hundreds of people as they pushed and stumbled against each other to obtain the best possible seats, those directly in the path of ubiquitous black television cameras. An aura of expectancy and envy pervaded the space. The air was suffused with a nauseating miasma of overpriced perfume, hairspray, and cologne (redolent of the most exclusive bordellos) and the unmistakable stench of bodies that had overpowered their underarm protection. This pungent mixture was occasionally seasoned with intermittent whiffs of smoke from Cuban cigars and cannabis.

The **communicants** were garbed each according to his or her gender. The males resembled a flock of over-stuffed penguins shoving each other off the ice. Their solemn raiment of black and white made it impossible to distinguish one from the other. The females, on the other hand, strove to be as unique as possible in their appearance, no two of them even closely resembling the other. They were encased in swaths of cloth of many hues, often semi-transparent and agleam with iridescence, spangles, ribbons, even feathers.

The colorful flock of females was in an unspoken competition to determine who could appear most attractive with the least possible coverage of her upper body. Most of the females could easily have qualified as honorary officers of the Deepest Possible Cleavage This Side of Indecent Exposure Society of America. One wonders about the magnitude of occurrence of bronchitis or pneumonia following these brazen displays on a freezing March night. They also could have been vying for the unannounced title of Dairy Queen of the Twenty-First Century.

The **ceremony** commenced. Lights flashed on and off, plebian music played intermittently, and outsized images of members of the congregation were cast upon the wall facing the communicants. Alternating with the performance of sacred hymns, a succession of prelates and virtual virgins took turns approaching and departing from the high altar.

With reverence, the people on the altar unfolded small pieces of parchment containing scripture. Hearing the words of the almighty exhorted the assembled penguins and escorts-of-the-night to waves, rather tsunamis, of frenzy. Chosen ones would emerge from the mass of excited worshippers and ascend the altar platform. There they were embraced by the virgins and the priests. To a crescendo of approving sounds from the watching hundreds, a small replica of the golden idol was thrust into their trembling hands.

Simultaneously the uncalled ones in the audience opined in reverent silence, "How about me? I'm so much better than they are. Talent be damned, receiving that damn statue would make me a first-rank celebrity, rich enough to buy a second custom Mercedes, put in an in-ground swimming pool for our third home, and buy my own Lear jet. High-level people in the industry would humbly beg me to work for them."

Immediately after receiving their miniature statue, the selected ones fell into a stupefying trance, wherein they chanted a plethora of ritual phrases of gratitude to the temple, to their beloved ones, to their cats and dogs, to their attorneys and accountants, to their crippled grandparents, to their upstairs maids, to their gynecologists and/or urologists, to their plastic surgeons, and to a special group of fellow worshippers.

The rite lasted for hours as each priest or virgin intoned the **sacred syllables**, "…and the winner is…"

Habitation of the Future

A high-caloric cityscape looms.
The circular capital with its red
roof rears itself far above
mundane surrounding structures
a fraction of its size. The pretzel-stick
legislators lie around at random
angles, contemplating how much salt
should be in the environment.

A garden behind the capital, flat as a board,
contains a rectangular cheddar-orange
flower bed. Abandoned white rakes
indicate the gardeners are on break
and are heading, no doubt, directly
to the cylindrical fast-food emporium
specializing in cayenne-laced brownies.

The square sky-blue pond adjacent
to the food emporium is frequented
by blasé workers sailing paper boats
made from classified documents.

A block or two away, the town water
tower stands with an orange roof
protecting it from souvenirs of low-flying
pigeons. The water, aerated and lemon-scented,
provides the town an excuse to charge
inhabitants exorbitant fees.

Diagonally behind the capital building
the ultra-modern aluminum-clad
cathedral nestles, reflecting both
the luminosity of a higher power
and the darkness of sinister forces
lurking within its architectural folds.

Hangman

Noah Webster, bored with his life on "the other side," seeks a few literate companions to help him try the prototype of a word game he has just invented. To give the game some teeth, he approaches both the Lord and Lucifer to join him. Each possesses the power to mete out the rewards or punishments called for in the new game. After the supreme rulers of heaven and hell consent to play in good faith and to eschew supernatural tricks, the trio agrees to meet the following Saturday evening (none of them happens to have a date) at seven o'clock on Noah's cloud. It is to be a BYOB event. The Lord chooses spiked nectar, Noah opts for hot-buttered rum, and Lucifer brings a keg of cayenne-flavored Jolt.

After greeting his guests, Noah lays out the rules for the new game, Hangman. It is played with the help of a sheet of papyrus, some ink, and the sharpened feather of a molting putto. One player chooses a word, which is not disclosed to the other players. The person selecting the secret word draws a simplified outline of gallows on a sheet of papyrus. Below the picture, he prints the initial and the final letters of the word he has in mind and connects them with a series of dashes, each dash representing one of the missing letters. The following is an example of how he sets up a game using, let us say, "columbine" as the mystery word.

C _ _ _ _ _ _ E

The other two players take turns guessing which letters might fit in the blanks. If the guessing player is correct, that letter is placed over its proper dash in the word, and the player may take another turn. If a letter appears more than once in the word, that letter is added in every position where it should be. If the guessed letter is not in the word, the player loses his turn and the chooser begins to draw a stick figure of a man hanging from the gallows. The first incorrect guess creates a hat, the second a head, the third a torso, the fourth and fifth respectively an arm, and the sixth and seventh a leg. See the following diagram.

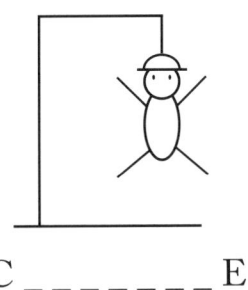

C _ _ _ _ _ _ E

The game ends when the word is correctly guessed by a player or when the figure of the "hangee" is completed. If the stick figure is completed before the word is guessed, the chooser is the winner. When a player makes an incorrect guess, he must punish some one (dead or alive) whose name begins with that incorrect letter. Every time a guess is fruitful, the successful player bestows a special gift on a person the initial letter of whose name is the same as the correctly-guessed letter.

The trio tries an experimental round. As the inventor of the game, it is agreed that Webster should be the first chooser of the secret word. He selects the word "columbine." The Lord leads off, prays to himself for luck and wisdom, and says "B." "You are in luck and now you may go again. But first, to whom will you extend a special gift?" "Hmm. I've got it. I will give Luther Burbank an eternal green thumb. The landscaping around here hasn't changed since the Garden of Eden went to seed and it certainly can use a lot of improvement. Besides, Burbank just hangs around day and night strumming his out-of-tune harp."

For his next turn, the Grand Designer of the Universe tries "G." "Sorry, Lord. Not this time." Webster then draws a hat at the end of the rope on the diagram. As a consequence of failing to guess correctly, the Lord must punish some one. He regretfully informs Johannes Gutenburg that books are rapidly becoming passé and his name and invention will soon be completely forgotten. Distant cries of "Ach, Himmel, nein!" can be discerned and then gradually fade away.

Lucifer's brow furrows as he takes his turn. After an eternity of hesitation, he opts for "A." "Hot shot, you goofed!" declares Webster as he adds a head to the stick figure. Lucifer's scarlet face breaks into an evil leer. He decides to demote Archimedes to the rank of doddering, two-bit mechanical hack. "Who in hell cares these days about levers and specific gravity and all that other scientific crap anyway? People don't want to bother their heads thinking and calculating. It is so much easier to leave that to their laptops."

The game continues apace as the participants become more and more enthusiastic not about correctly guessing the mystery word, but about the blessings and punishments they may freely dole out. God (heaven be praised) in his next turn selects "O" and upon being declared victorious, levitates up and down, tugs at his unruly beard, and triumphantly orders the pope to elevate Oprah (though still among the living) to immediate sainthood.

The Lord, now on a roll (as the ultimate Holy Roller), names in order "L" and "N." Firstly he beneficently grants Martin Luther eternal relief from his centuries-old constipation and then presents Richard Nixon with an electric shaver that actually works. For some ungodly reason, though, he next chooses "X" and loses his turn on the spot. Disappointed, he substitutes the nickname "Xmas" for the full designation for the celebration of the birth of his alleged son. The degrading popularization of "Christmas" will prove upsetting to academic linguistic purists in perpetuity.

Satan next gazes devilishly at the mystery word and cries out "M." Before taking his earned second turn, the horned-and-tailed creature requests a brief time out to scratches an itch under his beard and then opts to erase the reputation of the revolutionary author of *Das Kapital*, the patron saint of communism. Lucifer relegates dour Karl to be known forever only as the oldest, fifth, and funniest of the Marx brothers. His second choice is the letter "P." A torso is added to the hanging figure. Lucifer takes advantage of his free opportunity to punish someone again by making Alexander Pope lose his flair for rhyming as well as the poet's ability to compute an even five iambs per line. Additionally, the devil forces Pope to have compassion for the reader and occasionally skip a line or two on the densely-packed pages of his poems.

God looks upon the almost-completed word and in his infinite wisdom realizes that, at this point, the word can attain fulfillment merely through the addition of appropriate vowels. Early in the game, "A" proves to be incorrect and "O" and "E" already have niches in the secret word. In a rush, the all-knowing One sees the light and proclaims in turn "U" and "I." The Lord God, aka Jehovah aka Adonai, aka the Almighty, is the acclaimed victor (even though he has no idea what in heaven "columbine" means.) For one of his two sanctioned gifts, the deity decides to allow Ulysses, should he be inclined to repeat his epic voyage, to complete the Troy-to-Ithaca journey in a mere ten days in lieu of an entire decade, with the proviso, however, that the heroic Greek warrior remain true to Penelope and not screw around on his way home. All that remains is the gift for the letter "I." The winner ponders for an eon or two and then generously offers Icarus unlimited use of Helicopter One or, at least, a powered hang glider, should the hapless youth wish to attempt another journey to the sun. As an extra bonus, Icarus also receives an open-ended coupon, eternally valid for gratis advice from NASA.

The players conclude that the game is a huge success and will have universal appeal. However, they are still trying to arrive at a consensus regarding the most profitable way to market it.

In the Bathroom

I can still vividly see myself as a very young girl, perched
on the toilet seat lid late on a Sunday morning, raptly
watching my father as he put himself together to face
the day. I especially enjoyed the shaving ritual. I loved
to watch as he swirled and then gathered up the requi-
site amount of foam from the shaving cream mug with
his brush. Then he deftly maneuvered the white bub-
bles across his cheeks, over his upper lip and around
and under his chin. I don't recall whether he ever used
a straight razor. (He was a very cautious person.) I sat
entranced as he removed soap and bristle from his face
in sure, swift strokes. Oh, yes, there was the necessity
to adhere a bit of toilet paper to the occasional nick. I
remember the fascination of wondering how the bits of
paper stayed on his wounded face as each piece of tissue
morphed into a tiny Japanese flag.

My dad was not blessed with an excessive growth of head
hair. He had a pronounced widow's peak and kept the
rest cut very short. He always rubbed in Vitalis, an oily
hair dressing redolent of alcohol and strong antiseptic, to
keep his modest strands in place. I have no recollection
of his hair ever being mussed up. Additionally, the Vitalis
produced a patent leather sheen on his head.

For many years the flat we lived in was very meagerly
supplied with heat. In the winter months I was quite
reluctant to bathe. When I finally had to, I filled the
tub with scalding hot water and tentatively immersed

myself in it, one par-boiled toe by par-boiled toe. Once in the tub, I did enjoy its sensual warmth. Since my bathing was done at infrequent intervals, a scum of murky soap was left floating on the surface of the water. A quick shower removed it from my body, but the body of the tub always required much scrubbing. This was in the pre-detergent days and I suppose the water was hard to boot. As I dried myself off in the rapidly cooling room, I still recall with chagrin a layer of dirt or shed skin particles rolling off me onto the towel.

I remember my mother getting dressed in the bathroom. She first put on her armor, a formidable corset full of metal stays and laces and topped it with a brassiere (much too massive to be termed a bra). The brassiere overlapped the corset by about ten inches and hooked onto it on all sides. The back of the brassiere was fastened by eight or nine hooks and eyes. My mother's foundation was rapeproof and made her seem like a cross between a gladiator and a toreador.

In that same bathroom, at age eleven, I was horrified to discover blood in the toilet bowl after I had urinated. I ran to tell my mother who, instead of being concerned and nurturing, broke into a celebratory grin. How could she have been so joyous about the onset of what turned out to be forty painful years of *the curse*?

For ten years my husband and I lived in a house with a long, narrow bathroom. The toilet was by a window that always leaked cold air. It was necessary to sit on my hands to gradually warm up the seat whenever I had to use the toilet. Since he stood up most of the time, my husband had little compassion for my complaints. I even suspect that the occasions when he needed to sit down were timed to be immediately after I had abdicated the throne; he was living off my drained body heat. We were forever hounding each other to relinquish the sink or the toilet. If I was at the sink, he had to push past me to reach the toilet and vice versa. This threat to our marital tranquility was finally overcome when we retired and acquired a house with two full bathrooms and, best of all, double bathroom sinks. At last, a sink of my own.

Luddite

I fear technology, high, low or middle,
give it its due, genuflect in awe at its
ingenuity, but cringe helplessly
at its onward thrust, every moment
waxing more obsolescent, begetting newer,
ever more complex, counterintuitive offspring.
Just when I glean enough to wend my way
through arcane buttons and switches, black
boxes and power strips, a new version,
a new operating system, a new set of icons emerges,
followed by overblown instruction manuals,
maliciously written in prehistoric Sanskrit
by illiterate Martian idiots.

Montreal Expo—Summer of '67

We decided to drive up to Canada's Expo world fair, and spend a week there. We had heard and read how Canada had put together a wonderful fair to outdo all others in daring architecture, innovative exhibit techniques, and efficient arrangements to make a visit there a comfortable and memorable one. Well, it was memorable.

We contacted the official Expo housing office in Montreal and made reservations to stay, for a moderate price, in a suburb just outside of the city proper. Lodging was at a premium. Armed with maps and our reservation acknowledgment, we arrived, road weary, in the late afternoon. When we saw our place of lodging, we thought "time warp" or at least "geography warp."

Adjacent to a six-lane, high speed tangled intersection of major highways, we found our home away from home. It resembled an African village. There was a large old main building which housed communal toilet and shower facilities in its basement. Row after row of sinks, shower stalls, toilet booths, and primitive changing cubicles greeted us. The sleeping quarters erected by the enterprising owner of the property were crowded into his back yard. They comprised a dozen or more cylindrical huts, made of unpainted plywood, with conical roofs. Each hut was divided into quarters to provide accommodations for four parties per hut. Our slice of the pie was grandly furnished with a mattress on a platform on the floor, one chair, and a miniscule table, no windows. We were shocked and somewhat outraged at what was provided for the not inexpensive rent. When we tried to protest, we were met with a Gallic shrug and told we were lucky to find anyplace at all to stay.

Resigned to our fate, we tried to think of it as Canadian boot camp. When we started to unpack, we realized that there was no place for our clothes—no dresser and of course no closet. I considered it a triumph of international diplomacy when I managed to obtain some nails and a hammer from the proprietor. We drove the nails into the studs in our quarter of a hut and hung our things from them. It was the only bit of decoration in that luxurious hostelry.

Luckily we were so exhausted after 12 hours of doing the fair each day that we practically fell into a coma each night when we returned to the hut. The first night we could not sleep well because we kept hearing 18-wheelers and other vehicles roaring outside our thin wall as if they were about to drive through the hut. We were able to move to a quieter hut further inland from the highway for the balance of the week

Only a one-person-wide strip of sidewalk and waist-high fencing separated the hut compound from the busy highway. Mornings all the guests would traipse from hut to toilet facilities wearing pajamas and robes, towels on arm, soap and toothpaste in hand. It was like a nightmare sequence, a parade of displaced persons. In retrospect, we can laugh about it. Breakfast was available, for an additional fee. The double doors of the garage next to the main building rose up each morning to reveal an ad hoc short order counter. The hut refugees milled around the counter shouting out their orders. Convenient, but chaotic. It served up the loosest scrambled eggs I ever had to ingest.

One good feature of our opportunistic place of lodging was that it was a very short walk from the subway system, which took us to the heart of Expo. When I think of that tiring but exhilarating week in June 1967, I can still visualize our African village and smell the fragrance of its freshly cut plywood. Would I repeat the trip if Montreal hosted another Expo? You bet!

A More-Than-Modest Proposal

In an article in the March 1, 2009 issue of *The Progressive Populist*, Dr. Roberto Rodriguez, a research associate in Mexican American Studies at the University of Arizona, describes the failure of the recent Bush administration to deal with the immigration question along our southern border. He decries its great cost in dollars and in human suffering. "An examination of the Bush immigration policies will show that such an approach was not simply a massive drain on the national budget, but that it does not produce any wealth…Nothing symbolizes Bush's failure more than the walls/fences along the US/Mexico border."

Rodriguez further states that only 669 miles of our extensive border with Mexico have been fenced, at a cost since 2006 of almost $3 billion. He questions the utility of such fencing while leaving the balance of the border open. He states, "…the walls are tragic-comic and appear to be anachronistic." Further he describes the monumental (and extremely expensive) prison system and sham trials that have grown up as a result of the attempt to thwart immigration. Thousands of would-be immigrants--men, women and children--are being imprisoned and then deported.

Rodriguez suggests that President Obama "…examine not simply the immigration raids, the detention facilities and the sham trials, but also the entire premise of his predecessor's fear-based immigration and border enforcement policies." Right now the new president has a plethora of urgent national problems to cope with. To help him deal with his heavy presidential agenda, I respectfully propose the following solution to the immigration question.

The Federal Government should immediately establish a new national park along the fence, and indeed, along the entire length of the border with Mexico. The United States, with the cooperation of Mexico, would declare the border a locale to indulge in an exciting new sports activity--the licensed hunting and shooting of would-be immigrants. This would solve multiple problems for each country.

Local municipalities bordering on the park, along with the National Park Service, could charge a fee for the opportunity to gun down these unique moving targets. The National Rifle Association could provide free publicity, inviting its thousands of members to head south to enjoy a novel experience and to bring their spouses and children with them. Specific park areas would be set aside for hunters using each kind of weapon--shotguns, rifles, or crossbows. The use of grenades and assault weapons would involve higher fees and their own site. The fenced/walled areas would be altered to provide openings through which the shooters could safely aim their weapons. The unfenced stretches would be off limits to the shooters. These stretches would be used by the armed forces as an area for concentrated around-the-clock artillery, bombing and strafing practice.

Establishing the new park would provide many economic advantages both to the national government and to the border towns. Ninety percent of the shooting fees would go directly into the U. S. Treasury. Shooting ranges for municipal law enforcement personnel and for members of the armed forces could be shut down, and the police and armed service members sent to the new park to hone their skills and at the same time enjoy a little rest and recreation. The presence of the park and its unusual attraction would be an irresistible magnet for tourists (who would, of course, be charged an observer's fee).

The influx of shooters and tourists would stimulate the construction of motels, restaurants, theaters, gas stations, supermarkets, souvenir shops, houses of carnal comfort, and other establishments needed to support them. Souvenir shops, for example, could offer pieces of bullet-riddled, bloody clothing as well as 3-D images of immigrants attempting to dash to safety. The buildup along the border would create hundreds, if not thousands, of new jobs, providing revenue for both municipal and federal coffers through sales taxes, potential income taxes, etc.

The national government could eliminate the extremely high cost of operating courts and prisons established to handle massive illegal immigration. In fact, prison inmates throughout this country, regardless of the nature of their crime, could be offered the option of running the gauntlet in the reverse direction. Those who survive would have the option of remaining in Mexico to become teachers of English as a second language or to return to the United States to be trained as bankers or politicians.

To help mitigate its internal problems, the Mexican government would encourage their poor and unemployed to try their luck at running the gauntlet of bullets, arrows, and grenades. At random intervals during each day and night, there would be a cease-fire period of two or three hours to offer would-be immigrants a more even playing field. Any Mexicans who make it safely across the border's no-man's land would be permitted to remain in the United States as documented aliens with the proviso that they submit to the implantation of an electronic device that would permanently follow their movement throughout the country.

Yet another advantage to this proposal would be the opportunity to negotiate a pact with Mexican drug dealers, known to be experienced marksmen, to allow them to join the shooters free of charge and to establish retail outlets along the border for their wares. This would reduce rampant drug war violence and lower the cost of drugs. The anticipated geometric growth in volume of their business would compensate the drug lords for the loss of higher prices. The lure of inexpensive legal drugs would attract additional thousands of people to visit the border outlet stores. A portion of the resultant sales would be divided between the United States and Mexico.

A further source of income would be the harvesting of body parts, especially eyes, hearts and kidneys, from those who could not successfully reach the United States. This would be very profitable work for surgeons from both countries, who happened to graduate in the bottom tenth of their medical school classes, and would solve the urgent need for usable body parts. All shooters would be required to undergo special training to learn how to avoid harvestable portions of the body.

Unwanted or damaged internal organs would become grist for pet food factories. Other body parts could be converted into inexpensive ground meat for tacos and hamburgers. McDonald's and Taco Bell in both the United States and in Mexico have already exhibited great interest in this aspect of the proposal. As an additional bonus, ground-up bones could be sold to agricultural supply firms for use in enriching the soil.

To help publicize the park, there would be a naming competition, to be judged by a disinterested country. The park would bear the winning name in both English and in Spanish. A few suggested English names are Grisly National Park, Ammo-Amity National Recreation Area, or Green-Card Gauntlet National Monument.

In conclusion, this proposal would be a most effective means to control the rampant illegal immigration plaguing our country. Until the program achieves its ultimate purpose, it would be a boost to the economy, save the lives of thousands of patients in need of new eyes, hearts, or kidneys and enhance the worldwide reputation of our nation.

If the proposed enterprise turns out to be as successful as expected, an international long-range planning commission might include the establishment of a similar park along the border with Canada. Indeed, at this very moment, we are awaiting a tentative response from Ottawa.

My Name

Call me Annette. Everyone does, even my grandchildren, actually step-grandchildren. Hardly anyone addresses me as Mrs. Corth. It's too formal and we live an informal existence.

Annette is the French diminutive of Ann, little Ann. But I am a big person, always was. So I don't think of the literal meaning of my name. It's just my identifier. I like the name Annette. I enjoy its sound and its look, the repeated letters and especially the presence of the E's. I am pleased that it is a rather uncommon name, not a Mary or a Judy or a Shirley. When I hear someone call out *Annette*, I always turn around since there is very seldom another person with my name.

How did I come by the name? I come from a tradition that names babies after deceased people. I was to be named for my paternal grandmother, who died years before I was born. Her name was Hannah Eta, which loosely translates into English names beginning with an A and then an E. My mother tried out various combinations and was planning to settle on Audrey Elaine. I am so grateful that her sister intervened with another suggestion. Audrey Elaine seems too delicate for the tomboy I turned out to be and I still consider it a rather wimpy name. My aunt proposed Annette, Ann for the Hannah part and ette for the Eta unit. Sold! I was given no middle name. I am an NMI.

Yes, I had a nickname. I cringe now when I think of it. I was called Butzy. I don't know why. But it sounds like it was meant to be Butchy, which I resented. I was a clumsy child and often was teased about being more like a boy than a girl.

A is for anger. Anger filled many of my childhood years. Anger at my hairy, acned appearance. Anger at my lack of social graces. Anger at my mother for trying to rectify my shortcomings. Anger at my father for giving preference and special privileges to my younger brother. Anger at being friendless even though I rejected overtures from my peers.

N is for the nose job I had at age 26 after a broken romance. The short, cute nose was supposed to change my looks, my attitude, and my appeal to men. It worked. Ten years later I met and married my husband. He could not have cared less about the size, shape, or angle of my nose.

N is for Naomi, my favorite cousin. For years I envied her good looks and vivacity. She was a magnet for young men and skilled at flirting with them. She married several years before I did and I felt worthless in comparison to her. Fate plays interesting tricks. Her husband was sickly and died young. She had a number of ill-starred affairs, got involved with drugs, and had a nervous breakdown. My marriage has endured over 35 years and is very happy. Fortunately Naomi has found herself and has a satisfying existence. She and I are best friends and share painting and poetry-writing interests with each other on a regular basis.

E is for efficiency in tasks given to me, for eagerness to learn, for excellence in my professional work and in my retirement pursuits. E is for English, my love of words, puns, puzzles.

T is for talent in visual and verbal arts. T is for the tenderness toward my cats that I am not able always to extend to people. T is for temperature. I like it cold. Winter is a time of great invigoration for me. I cannot tolerate the heat of summer. I long for an ice age and not for global warming.

T is for my tongue which wags incessantly. T is for the taste of ethnic foods. Eating, especially in restaurants, is a great source of pleasure to me, beyond its role in sustenance.

E is for eye and ear. I revel in the sights of nature and in the excitement of art museums and galleries. Ear is for my great love of classical music of all kinds, especially vocal music. Opera, oratorios, and requiem masses energize my soul. When I paint, I always play music.

New Olympic Event

Hello, sports lovers, Peter Prick along with Vulva Kuntt here in Bangkok, Thailand, site of the 2014 summer games. Exotic Bangkok, world famous for its love affair with love affairs, is the perfect locale for the finals of this exciting new Olympic event that we are covering for you this afternoon--team intercourse. We will describe the ins and outs of all the action including the pageantry of the entrance of the athletes, their colorful uniforms, and the intricate rules of a fascinating new sport, new to the Olympics, that is. The preliminary rounds of this event have received very meager media coverage, but we are compensating for that today. Every last seat in Orgee arena is filled with spectators, panting from a combination of the oppressive climate and their barely-controlled anticipation, while refreshing themselves with frozen K-Y-filled chocolate candy bars, dildo burgers with blue cheese, G-spot peppermint balls, and leather-and-whip sweetened ice tea, all local specialties.

Once again, the temperature hovers in the upper nineties and the humidity has reached an overwhelming 89 percent. To provide a measure of protection for various usually-covered, delicate parts of the contestants, a purple silken canopy has been erected high above the mattress-covered playing field. Gentle ocean breezes billow the canopy into voluptuous shapes, casting a subtle aura of languid movement over the entire arena. Just below the canopy there is an array of enormous TV screens to assure that all spectators have an intimate view of every facet of the game.

This new sport has become extremely popular around the globe. Top-notch players are idolized as national heroes. Team intercourse competitions are replacing the popularity of bullfighting in Spain and Latin America, reindeer racing in Lappland, and unisex soccer in the Vatican. Standard innocuous "family life" classes in middle schools have been replaced by film clips of each country's national team as the athletes practice basic coital positions and choreograph new movements. Pre-pubescent boys and girls proudly hang over their beds explicit posters of their heroes in action, fashion jewelry out of empty K-Y tubes to wear as talismans, and vie for roles as cheerleaders for their home town teams. In art, science, and health classes the young people learn to design costumes appropriate for the sport and practice how to locate the erogenous zones of their classmates.

Today's match for the gold medal is between Germany and Israel, both of whom have taken a pre-competition oath to "let bygones be bygones." The German team is known as the Huns and the Israeli team, the Dreidels. Each team wears uniforms representing its national colors--red, gold, and black for the Huns and white and blue for the Dreidels. At great expense, top design-ers and textile engineers around the world have created spectacular but functional outfits for the players. More details about the outfits themselves later. On the back of the German uniforms, the Huns have inscribed their team motto, "Fucken macht frei." The Dreidels display two mottos across their backs, "Chosen people" and "Never again!" In addition, to reflect their origin as a pastoral people, the Dreidels have emblazoned "Screw ewe!" across both cheeks of their hind quarters. The members of the German team are Hans Schlange, Hans Stange, Hans Putz, Irmgard Grossbrust, Irmgard Labia, and Irmgard Kasten. The Israeli players are Abraham Knesset, Isaac Sabra, and Jacob Kosher. Their teammates are Rachel Einstein, Ruth Zweistein, and Rebecca Dreistein.

To help defray the costs of training, travel, uniforms, etc., each team in the final medal round is allowed to sign on with its very own sponsors, ranging from distributors of Gideon bibles containing illustrations of begetting, multi-colored sex toys, and aphrodisiac underarm deodorants to chocolate-flavored clitoral stimulants, effervescent spermicides, erectile dysfunction balms, and illuminated masturbation manuals. Additionally, some other sponsors are leading food producers such as Germany's Siegfrieds Sauerkraut und Wurst Salsa and Dachau-Auschwitz Gas Oven Doughnuts as well as Israel's PLO-Style Frozen Falafel and Minyan Brothers Mandelbrot and Matzohs. The closer a team gets to the final round of the competition, the more sponsors are garnered. No corporation wants to back a loser.

Now a review of the rules of play. No substitution or replacement is allowed for injured or penalized participants. At all times, each coital position assumed must involve the entire team. No more than two minutes may elapse without team members being in intimate physical contact with at least one other person. A limit of four minutes of foreplay precedes the main coupling. There is no restriction on various gender combinations, vocal emissions, or the utilization of any available bodily orifice. Use of sex toys is optional.

There are a number of caveats for which penalties or expulsion from play may be in order. All participants must have current certificates attesting to the fact that they have been drug-free for the past six months—no steroids, no erectile stimulants, no birth control pills, no multivitamins. Condoms are optional, and if they choose to, female athletes may use diaphragms. Premature ejaculation or loss of erection is ground for immediate expulsion from the competition. In such cases, the balance of the team must carry on with reduced numbers. Medals are awarded on a provisional basis. One month after the game, the female athletes are checked for impregnation. If they have missed a period, their team loses the contest.

Umpires from a neutral country, Tibetan monks in today's contest, will enter carrying six-foot long Tibetan horns and an over-size brass gong. For the game itself, they will be provided with official digital cameras and electronic chronometers to constantly monitor all moves--in and out, up and down--that the players may make. Images from the cameras are immediately flashed onto the giant television screens positioned around the perimeter of the stadium. What the umpires see is what the spectators see. This is a very democratic sport.

The pageant is about to begin. First we hear the rousing notes of "Fanfare for the Common Man" played by the brass and percussion sections of the Olympic International Orchestra. Next comes the entrance of the participants. The procession is led by the four umpires attired in saffron and gold robes. Behind them prance four nubile cheerleaders carrying the digital cameras and electronic chronometers on scarlet velvet cushions. They in turn are followed by medical teams wearing white satin scrubs and elbow-length rubber gloves. Each team invites its own gynecologist, urologist and proctologist to attend to injured team members.

Finally, accompanied by enthusiastic applause, here come the intercourse teams! To the strains of "Deutschland ueber Alles" the Huns enter the arena, arms interlocked, legs swinging high in rhythmic goose steps. Close behind them the Dreidels come into view, dancing to the notes of "Hatikvah" as they move down the field in an inside-out hora circle. All of the players are tall, slender, long-limbed, comely, graceful, and in excellent shape. The costumes worn by the Huns afford visible proof that the German athletes are all naturally blond. On the other hand, half of the Dreidel team exhibits 10-inch-long examples of first-rate treatment by Israel's most skillful mohels. The other half of the Israeli team flaunts pectoral splendor measuring at least 46D.

A few words are in order at this point about the uniforms. The athletes are garbed in sleek, absorbent, glistening body suits made of a secret blend of material, enabling them to slink along each other's bodies with a minimum of friction. As mentioned before, the abstract design of the outfits highlights the colors of the respective national flags. Because the rules of the game forbid the removal or addition of any article of clothing during the competition, the garments have been engineered by a group of top physiologists and choreographers to possess large apertures in the chest region of the women's outfits, allowing complete availability of basic mammary structures. For both genders the uniforms come equipped with long narrow openings running the entire length of the crotch region, ventral and dorsal, to enhance viewing and to facilitate access. In an attempt to be economical, material excised from the tights has been used to create the minimal costumes worn by the cheer leaders.

After the four minutes of foreplay, each team must assume a variety of group positions and patterns with all team members remaining in constant contact with at least one other person. Each side is to perform two obligatory patterns. The Huns chose to form a rotating swastika and a foaming beer stein, while the Dreidels plan to arrange themselves in a scintillating Star of David and a blazing menorah. Points are awarded for artistic merit as well as for accuracy in not exceeding the two minutes allowed for changing from one formation to another. The main objective of the game, for which 69 bonus points are awarded, is to achieve unison culmination within twenty minutes.

To express good will and sportsmanship, the members of each team must saunter through a gauntlet of the members of the opposite team, caressing or kissing their choice of protruding organ. With alternate cheers of "Go! Go!" and "Come! Come!" the cheer leaders bring the eager spectators to their feet, inducing them to gratify themselves through their sweat-drenched clothes. The umpires give three blasts on their horns and simultaneously strike the brass gong.

Let the games begin!

Ninety-Five

Now 81, I aspire to reach 95,
at which time I'll serenely float off
in a flood of soy sauce, molten
milk chocolate, cabernet sauvignon,
and sour-cream-embellished cold borscht.

Mother drifted away at ninety-three,
her fault. She eschewed soy sauce,
chocolate, and most red wine.
Borscht alone could not help.

How do I reach one hundred,
a rounder age than ninety-five?
Perhaps a robust boost of garlicky
bouillabaisse, succulent pad tai,
a boatload of sashimi supreme,
a two-pound sea-water-boiled lobster,
an entire chocolate fudge cake.

Obsession

Food, toujours food. Music can be resonant, art color-ful, exercise life-prolonging, sex OK in its place, reading enlightening, but, ah, food, food—exciting, seductive, sensual, and in the end, broadening. How delightful that something necessary for mere existence can entice on so many levels.

Wallow in the aroma of mulled cider, sautéed garlic and onions, pizza, Thai anything, brownies baking, roast lamb beckoning. Revel in the spectrum of textures—the crunch of croutons, the palate-adhesion of peanut butter, the slither of buttered linguini, the gentle caress of mashed potatoes, the resistance of squid, the bounce of jello.

Luxuriate in the visual radiance of golden squash reclin-ing on forest green spinach alongside shimmering scar-let tomato slices, perhaps accented with the gleam of a black olive or two. Behold the rare roast beef, its red interior merging into pink into the sepia brown of its crust. Watch the flow of the au jus as it lovingly deco-rates a field of alabaster potatoes enhanced by snippets of verdant dill.

Feast the ears on the sound of a Brunswick stew gently simmering or the sizzle emanating from a pan of crisp-ing bacon or the heavy plop of chocolate pudding as it thickens.

Why is it so difficult for a sensible person like me to elude obesity? Who made food so damn appealing? This comestible obsession dominates my being. It overpowers my will and intellect in its headlong rush toward satisfaction; but it is never satisfied. I love and hate my obsession, adore its pleasure-giving and fear its control over me. Give me more food, more, again and again.

Obsession.

A Perfect Day

begins with the insistent purr of the cat,
begging for food, promising not to throw up.
I arise with eager vigor, free of rusted knees
and erosive gastric juices.
The hot shower water arrives
without dragging its drops.
My costume du jour matches
and craftily disguises my size.
I indulge in breakfast both
sumptuous and slimming.
Garrison Keillor reads my poems
for the tenth or twentieth time.
My somber spouse greets me
with a big smile and a warm hug.

Precious Gem

For quite some time I have been fantasizing about what I would put into a classified personal ad, not that I'm ready to get rid of my husband. But then it always pays to be prepared for an emergency. (We are almost finished with the cases of beans and tuna that we stockpiled for Y2K.)

Let's see now. How will I start it off? I have noticed that personal ads in the NEW YORK MAGAZINE seem to concentrate on the over-39 crowd these days. Maybe I should try to be honest, not openly so, but not flagrantly dissembling. OK, here goes:

Precious Gem. Well-ripened artist. Hm, sounds like I'm a rotten tomato. How about: *Well under 80 and still mobile.* That will let them know that I'm not a kid but am still sprightly, or at least non-arthritic.

Brown eyes (can't fudge that) and *salt and pepper hair* (heavy on the salt, light on the quantity of hair.) *Carries weight well, body mass less than 30.* Maybe that's too specific. I'll omit the body mass part. *Enjoyed most of my life at 5'7" and now gracefully consolidating.* That sounds intriguing.

No longer chooses to concentrate on downhill skiing, backpacking into the wilderness, polar-bear swimming, or bungee jumping. That will give me an aura of having been athletic and daring but finally having come to my senses. *Financially secure, retired early.* No mention that I retired early in 1985 or that my wealth comes from Social Security and my meager library pension.

Seeking healthy (no by-passes, please) 60-65 year old male, tall (unconsolidated 5'11" or more), unattached, hirsute (on the top of the head), interested in intellectual intercourse, classical music, travel overseas, theatre, poetry (mine not yours) and contemporary art (will consider a 30% discount off any of my paintings you wish to acquire, in appreciation of your excellent taste.)

Will not burden you with home cooking, love elegant restaurants, especially ethnic cuisine. Cat lovers only need respond. No dogs, birds, snakes, ferrets or fish. No drugs, smoking, pungent cheeses or cheap wine.

Am intelligent, verbally playful, humorous and full of resolve. Prefer to win all discussions just to maintain a warm, non-competitive atmosphere where the man of my dreams can relax and let me make all the decisions about what to do, where to go, etc.

Don't pass up this rare jewel. Hurry and respond to Box IM4U before someone else finds me and sets me in his life and heart.

Prescription No. 203340

It's almost nineteen years to the day that we were pre-
scribed for Miss Isabel Chase, the poor old dear. Isabel
was 74 years old then, had several degenerative diseases,
and was an accomplished hypochondriac. She would
have received all sixes and a gold medal had the obsession with her health been an Olympic event.

Her physician, Dr. Asher, realized that combating her
hypochondria was hopeless. He therefore had Kline's
Pharmacy on North Aurora Street concoct us, a batch
of serious-looking placebo capsules, to calm her con-
cerns. The good doctor informed his oldest patient (she
had been bringing her complaints and worries to his office as regularly as the faithful go to confession) that he
had just learned about a breakthrough medication that
coordinated the body's various systems to fight physical attacks on them from within and without. He told
Isabel that extensive tests had revealed promising results
with no side effects other than an apparent increase
in appetite, eight hours per night of unbroken sleep,
infrequent nocturnal urination, and a surge in energy.
Patients taking the medication would feel impelled to
stretch their body often and to walk briskly at least an
hour a day.

We capsules were somewhat abashed at being party
to this benign deception, but we agreed that it was for
a worthwhile cause. We were pleased that we were
housed in a jazzy emerald-green square bottle, lending

an upbeat aura to the prescription. Green, after all, is a sign of spring, fresh hope, and renewal. Isabel kept our bottle on her dressing table, where the early morning sun rendered it a magical glow.

Our prescription was renewed fifteen times each year for almost twenty years. Isabel's visits to Dr. Asher diminished in frequency. At her semi-annual check-ups, she thanked the doctor profusely for his wisdom and gift of a new lease on life. In gratitude, she inundated him with home-made pies of every kind.

As her arthritis, headaches, shortness of breath, and dyspepsia subsided, she plunged into a surprising spectrum of creative activities. Every June she sent Dr. Asher photographs of her in her over-the-ankle sneakers and exercise garb, accepting a first-place medal for the annual senior citizen's walkathon. She developed an interest in the arts. Her poems were published in prestigious journals and her paintings were purchased by major museums. Each year she chaired four fund drives in town for various good causes. We were bemused at the power of our fraudulence. How could encapsulated cornstarch, sugar and a pinch of vinegar achieve such miraculous results?

Dr. Asher died of a sudden heart attack at the age of 55. In her 93rd year, on the anniversary of our first prescription, Isabel did not wake up in the morning. There was a smile on her face as though she could see the early rays of the sun turn our bottle into a sparkling square emerald.

Saturday Night in Sandstone Flats

The Sundowner Motel—what a dump!

On the way to Las Vegas our rental car decided to have a stroke. It suddenly shuddered, groaned and fell into complete paralysis, accompanied by a hissing cloud of evil-smelling vapor. We were in the great metropolis of Sandstone Flats, Nevada, late on a Saturday night. Sandstone Flats consisted of three bars, a combination general store/garage and the Sundowner Motel. The store/garage was dark and deserted so we ventured into the motel to learn whether there was anyone in town who could check out our moribund vehicle either right away or the next morning. No dice.

Monday afternoon the garage would be staffed and the resident mechanic, his skill limited mostly to pumping gas and changing tires, could give the car a look-see, if he were sober enough after his weekend in Vegas, 97 miles to the south. Obtaining a last-minute rental car was so far out of the question that the smarmy motel clerk broke into a loud, toothsome roar of laughter when we suggested it. There were no cars or cabs (another burst of guffaws) available in town, but the motel did have a vacant room.

The reception area of the motel was dimly lit and redolent of stale cigar smoke and even staler beer. We had had hopes of lounging in the decadent luxury of a Las Vegas hotel surrounded by plush décor and sybaritic accommodations. We flung a diabolic curse at our non-functional car and wearily checked into the Sundowner.

The motel was a downer regardless of the presence of the sun. Our room was small, appeared to be painted institutional green, and contained a double bed, a rust-stained sink (lacking a proper washer), several hangers on nails, a table with one drawer (no self-respecting Gideon would have left a Bible in it), and the world's loudest asthmatic window fan. No drapes, just a slightly ajar venetian blind missing several slats.

The bed linens appeared to have been fresh in the re-cent past. However, the threadbare towels seemed clean enough. The mattress boasted a semi-mountainous to-pography, which led us to believe it was not too virginal. The toilet was down the hall, to be shared by the four motel rooms. Luckily it was very quiet. We performed our nightly ablutions and warily lowered ourselves into the creaking bed. Exhausted, we quickly fell into an uneasy sleep.

Suddenly we were jarred awake by banging car doors, slamming screen doors, and raucous shouting. Most of the voices were masculine, but from time to time a woman would shout something that sounded like *Next!* or *Your time's up, Joe.* Cars drove up to the building, doors slammed, glass broke, and beds squeaked. Inebriated people yelled and cursed, more door slamming, knocks even on our door, cars driving away, etc. We soon real-ized we had not checked into the local convent.

Around 5 a.m. business seemed to slacken off. We dragged ourselves out of bed a few hours later and looked for a telephone to see if a cab or another rental car could come out to Sandstone Flats to rescue us. Yes, a cab could come for us from Las Vegas, for a price three times greater than the amount we planned to spend in the glittering casinos. The cab arrived late in the afternoon. Before we got into it, we thought we would check the rental car once more, just for the hell of it. We put the key into the ignition, engaged the starter, and reluctantly witnessed a mechanical resurrection. With a malevolent purr, the damn engine sprang to life.

Show Business

The meeting takes place in Jerusalem on a hot March afternoon, the eve of Purim, at a table in a small alcove near the rear of the Star-of-David-Bucks coffee house. An elderly man with disheveled long white beard and shoulder-length curly hair sits at the table, impatiently drumming his fingers. His garb is many centuries out of style. However, nobody pays attention to his dusty white robe trailing to the café floor, tied with a length of frayed rope, or to his unusual sandals. After all, Purim is celebrated with masquerades, and the old man is probably already dressed for a party that night.

At length, a short stocky man with a receding hairline and a crop of bushy hair enters the establishment and looks around as though searching for someone he does not know too well. The man's face is red and he is sweating profusely. No wonder, he is attired in a suit complete with vest, dress shirt, and bow tie more suitable for a merchant in Connecticut than for a visitor to Jerusalem. Suddenly his face registers a glimmer of recognition and he rapidly approaches the impatient old man.

Barnum: The prophet Moses, I presume. I thought I recognized you from your pictures and statues. Mighty hot climate you have here.

Moses: Barnum, what kept you so long? I'm very busy helping Jehovah design a few new plagues, just in case, and I can hardly spare the time to meet with you. By the way, forget the prophet part. I answer to plain Moses, Moishe, or Moe. What should I call you?

Barnum: Moe, feel free to address me as Barnum, Phineas, Phinny (that's what the little woman calls me), or P. T. will do. Thanks for agreeing to spare some time from your busy schedule to answer a few questions I have always had about your work and possibly to work out some business deals.

Moses: OK, P. T., what do you want to know? I thought you knew every trick in the scroll. So what specifically do you want from me? Here comes the waitress. Quite a looker, isn't she? Well-stacked! What would you like to drink? I can recommend the "two-cents-plain," light and bubbly, or what I am drinking, an egg cream. Don't look so puzzled. An egg cream contains neither eggs nor cream. It's a concoction of milk and chocolate syrup, spruced up with a shot of seltzer. House specialty.

Barnum: You sold me on that second one. Miss, I'll have an egg cream, please. Say, are there any more girls at home like you?

Moses: Come on. Let's get down to business.

Barnum: Moe, I'm a successful showman. I like to attract big audiences for my museums, zoos, and sideshows, but I am running out of new ideas. I thought, for example, your burning bush routine was terrific. How did you do it? Does it require any special kind of bush? Is there a secret coating to enable the fire to keep burning without hurting the bush? Is the process patented? I got plenty of money and would gladly compensate you for allowing me to include a burning bush trick in my new show.

Moses: Trick? That was no trick. Jehovah helped me stage that miracle to demonstrate to our people that He is the master of all nature.

Barnum: You could have fooled me, Moe. Can you tell me then how you pulled off all those plagues? Did you really take part in their design? I would love to know how you convinced the Egyptians that those frogs were real or that the water actually turned to blood. Wow, people would flock in from all over to feel they were experiencing some of the plagues, just the ones that didn't kill anyone or make them really sick, that is.

Moses: Is nothing sacred to you? The plagues were not called down from above for the amusement of tourists.

Barnum: OK, Moe. What about your wonderful phrase: *Let my people go?* I'd love to register that and lease it out to activists who are fighting the establishment. Is it available? For how much?

Moses: Sorry, P. T., that phrase is reserved for very special occasions.

Barnum: I got another idea, from which we might both profit. How do you feel about guided tours through the wilderness? Naturally, we would aim for just four days, symbolic, you know, of the full forty years. Where were you precisely when all of you were wandering around? Didn't you have any decent maps or trained scouts? You knew in general where you were headed, so why didn't you consult the local people or members of passing caravans? I am sure they must have known how to get to Canaan.

We could hire camels to carry customers and their luggage and to provide the proper atmosphere for the trip. I'm sure that many people from the fanatically-religious to the casual tourist would be eager to follow in your footsteps, so to speak, but in a more linear fashion. We could split the earnings fifty-fifty, dollars for me and shekels for you. Maybe we could use your picture on the trip literature.

Moses: What an outrageous idea!

Barnum: We have to do something about the food. Vacationers and pilgrims expect a decent, varied diet, none of this manna stuff. We could have the food catered, kosher of course, and offer delicious specialties of the region plus pizza for the Americans and the Italians, sauerbraten for the Germans, etc. By the way, Moe, what did manna taste like? Bland, spicy, salty, fruity? How could you put up with it day after day, year after year? A merciful god would not inflict that on his chosen people.

Moses: On second thought, your idea doesn't seem that bad. I'll check with Jehovah first. He might be able to furnish maps that hit all the highlights of the region in the four days. We may have to do a three-way split on the proceeds, however. He will probably want his share in sacrificed lambs.

Speaking of publicity, my informants tell me that you often, shall we say, stretch veracity to serve your own capitalistic ends. I want to check the tour posters and flyers you send out to make certain that you do not embellish the true nature of the tour.

Barnum: That's OK with me. I'm so glad you seem interested in the enterprise. After all, it does have an educational value.

Moses: Another thing, P. T., I do think it was shameful how you passed off that four-year-old boy as an eleven-year-old dwarf and toured around the world, calling him General Tom Thumb. And all those freaks! Don't you realize it is blasphemous to profit from Jehovah's design errors? Furthermore, there is no excuse, on top of exploiting those unfortunates, to try to fake some of their abnormalities. Have you no pride, no integrity?

Barnum: Just a minute, Moe. Those people were never forced to pretend to be what they were not. It was a living for them as well. And business is business.

By the way, I have always admired how you orchestrated that brilliant bit of pretending to go mountain climbing (good view from Mt. Sinai, isn't it?) and then returning with the two fragile clay tablets with all those unreasonable, supposedly God-given, commandments written on them? What a coup! Too bad you lost your temper when you came down and dropped them. If I could pull that off, I would use a better material than clay and try to keep my cool. How much do you want for letting me in on that secret?

Moses: That was no hoax. It was orchestrated between me and Jehovah. I never could understand why our people were so impatient and had to make and dance around that damned golden calf.

Barnum: And I could never comprehend the big fuss you made about the calf. It must have really been quite attractive. I would love to have one to include in my sideshow. Do you know whether there are any spares available? No? Too bad!

Moe, I see you are anxious to bring our meeting to a close. Before you go, I would greatly appreciate it if you would give me instructions for creating more Siamese twins. That was such a good come-on, and I was so disappointed when they passed away. OK, I see that you are unhappy about my request.

But I do have another question, Moe. How in the world did you bring off that spectacular Red Sea business? Was there a tsunami, a tidal bore, or a tornado? I don't think that civil engineering was sufficiently advanced in your time to accomplish parting of the waters on such a large scale. Maybe everyone was fooled into thinking a tunnel under the water was really the drained sea bottom.

Moses: What's wrong with you? Do you think everything is a trick?

Barnum: Moe, your face is all red and you are glaring at me like Vesuvius about to blow. Calm down. Keep cool. Your glass is empty. How about a refill? The drinks are on me. Alright, I guess you really have to go now. Thanks again for meeting with me. I really look forward to hearing if any of my propositions appeals to you.

Please, just one last question. Do you really have horns?

Snack Time

Three p.m., snack time. With a spring to her step, she left the bathroom and headed for the kitchen. A successful bathroom session, she calculated, deserves a bit of recklessness in her mid-day snack. The ongoing struggle to reconcile too much body with too much addiction to chocolate and nuts caused her to tense up and try to control every part of her body from eyes to hands to gut. She knew a thimbleful of an Almond Joy bar was the limit she had set for herself, but once again her craving for more and more—for the entire box of forbidden candy bars—tore at her resolve.

She tried to divert her longing to cram herself full of the brown and white delight by thinking of the advent of autumn and its release from the stultifying grip of heat and humidity. Perhaps a little exercise prior to having her snack would strengthen her ability to adhere to the necessary but detested dietary discipline.

She selected one of her favorite CD's, fifty minutes of intense African drumming and chanting. She put the disk on the CD player and turned it on. Alone in the house, she removed her shoes and outer garments and wrapped a large vividly-printed shawl around her ample hips. The incessant beat of the drums and the feral sounds of the chanting caught her up as she stomped and bent and gyrated to the music. She sensed a meld of captivity and freedom as she moved faster and faster to the compelling rhythms. She imagined she could inhale the scent of the sun-drenched savannah, the tall grasses, the rising dust, and the odor of bodies in exertion. As she twisted and jumped, her arms and legs would strike now the coffee table, now the edge of the bookcase. Enveloped in giving herself to the music, she seemed oblivious to the bruises and cuts she was sustaining.

Then it was over. The disk played itself out. Glistening with sweat and suddenly exhausted and faint, she staggered back to the bathroom, stripped off her clinging underwear, and all but fell into the shower. She braced herself against the tiled walls as torrents of cool water cascaded over her exhilarated but spent body. A great thirst seized her. Trailing the remnants of the shower behind her, she headed for the kitchen and the bottled water in the refrigerator. To her amazement, she consumed an entire quart in a series of compulsive gulps.

The wall clock confirmed that it was now half past four. She stood, water still running off her body, when the back door opened followed by an explosion of young boys. Her three sons had returned from their soccer practice and thundered into the kitchen seeking pre-dinner snacks. They froze into postures of surprise, shock, and then shame. There in a large puddle stood their mother. Her arms had black and blue patches and a trickle of red ran down one leg.

"Mom, are you OK?" "Did someone break in and attack you?" "Where are your clothes?" She reassured them that she was indeed safe and OK. The boys then inquired what might be available for a snack. The mother thought for a brief instant and then proffered a complete box of Almond Joy bars.

Staff of Life Electrical Stiffener with Aroma Generator (SOLESWAG)
Important! Read Before Commencing Operation

Congratulations! You have just purchased a Home Model No. 5130315 Staff of Life Electrical Stiffener with Aroma Generator. This product represents a triumph of symbiotic mechanical, materials, and electrical research and engineering. The machine incorporates the latest post-space-age materials to yield a device that is efficient, safe, and straightforward to operate. The following suggestions will maximize utilization.

Ascertain from NOAA's satellite output whether the local atmospheric conditions are favorable (no tornadoes or hurricanes forecast) prior to installing the SOLESWAG in the optimal specified manner, which is on a firm, flat surface (FFS) one meter above floor level and shows a positive coefficient of removal (COR) from any overhanging combustible object and is less than 1.25×10 to the 0th power meters distant from the nearest electron feeder station (EFS). Adjacent running dihydrogen oxide (H_2O) is definitely hazardous and should be avoided. (Figure 1.)

To prepare for efficient operation of the SOLESWAG, insert up to its hilt the (male) double-tined prong (DTP) at the distal terminus of the ion transport line (ITL) emerging from the dorsal panel of the SOLESWAG into the receiving (female) aperture of the EFS. The DTP may require rotating to fine tune it for effective orientation of the prongs with reference to the apertures of the EFS. (Figure 1.)

Select one or two appropriate samples of staff of life (SOL=TM=SOL) enumerated below, not exceeding the width and length of the opening of the parallel double elevator slots (PDES) located on the top of the SOLESWAG. Prior to activating the spring-loaded operation bar (SLOB) on the narrow side of the SOLESWAG, opposite the point of attachment of the ITL, the desired degree of stiffness (DDOS), which also controls the depth of coloration intensity (DOCI) and resultant aroma generation (RAG) of the treated material (TM=SOL=TM), must be established. Utilize the first three digits of the right hand to rotate the circular dial, located below the SLOB, to the numeric level representing the desired outcome (determined exclusively by experimentation and the nature of material selected). (Figure 1.)

The stiffness of the final product varies asymptotically from almost flexible without fracturing (AFWF) to catastrophic rupture upon manual bending (CRUMB). The spectrum of coloration (SOC) achieved can range from Arctic snow white (ASW) to Pennsylvania anthracite ebony (PAE). Suggested TM=SOL=TM includes white, whole wheat, rye, seeded rye, pumpernickel, bagel, and rectangular frozen waffle. Matzohs and crackers are to be avoided. They are not covered under the manufacturer's warranty.

After calculating the desired selections, insert one or two units of TM=SOL=TM into the PDES, being careful not to exceed one unit per slot. With the right fore finger, depress the SLOB, located below the DDOS, DOCI, and RAG dial with a minimum of one dyne of force, until the SLOB locks into position and emits an audible click (AC), optimally below 75 decibels. (Figure 1.) In the event of emergency, activate the stop operation bar (SOB) at the lowest level on the side of the SOLESWAG that contains the above-described controls. Activation of the SOB simultaneously produces an AC (if the temperature is lower than 113 degrees Celsius), terminates all operations, and causes the PDES to elevate the TM=SOL=TM at a significant fraction of the speed of light. Should the temperature exceed 113 degrees, a siren will sound and 911 will be electronically alerted.

If the control settings are too high to produce the desired outcome, aromatic fumes (AF) will emit a noticeable aroma of combustion (NAOC), frequently leading to the creation of choking black smoke (CBS) and eventually open flames (OF). In this case, it is important to secure sufficient ambient ventilation (SAV) to forestall asphyxiation.

Warning: During and immediately after conclusion of the operation, the SOLESWAG and TM=SOL=TM will be thermally elevated and should be handled with care. Refrain from inserting fingers, tongue or metal objects into the PDES at that time.

For assistance in dealing with any questions or technical problems involving the usage of SOLESWAG, telephone the Singapore Customer Service Department between two and four a.m. EST. Be prepared to have the cost of the call and the salary of the customer service representative billed to your credit card. To secure the services of an interpreter, with or without advanced EE and/or ME degrees, consult our current website www.soleswag.inscrutablyfutile.com.

FIGURE 1.

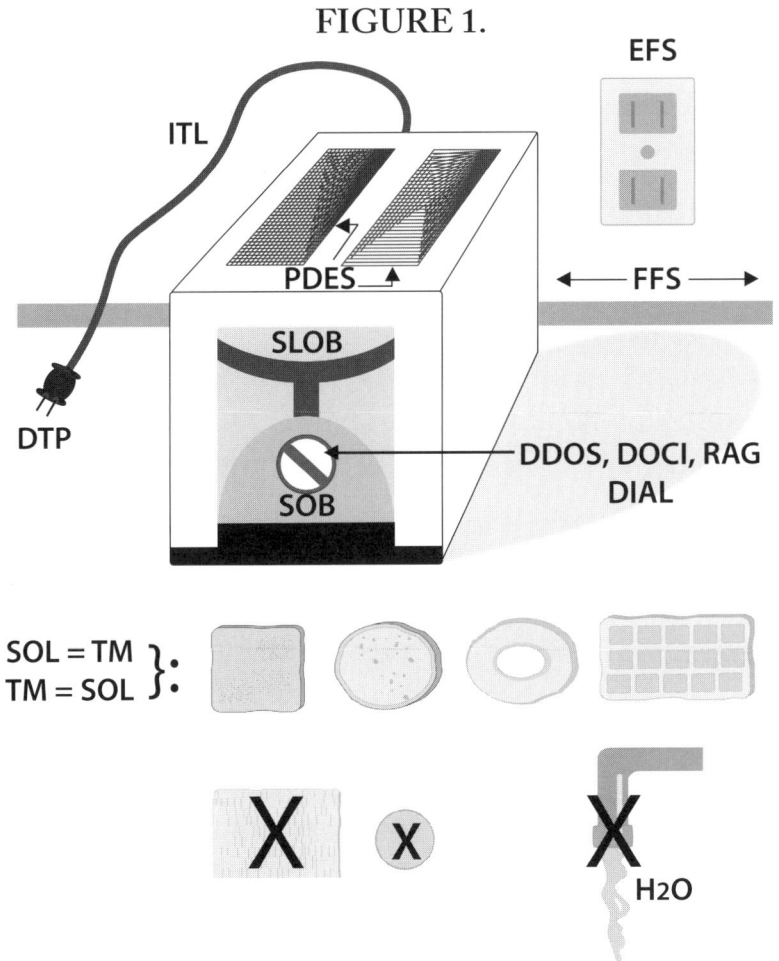

Starry Day

Turquoise hills undulate
beneath golden light
rising toward orange.
Somber silent clouds
embrace land and sky.
Misshapen stars, like
merciless throbbing strobes,
punctuate diurnal firmament.
Purple leafless trees witness
merger of twilight and dawn,
creating stellar détente.

Three Sisters

The Mother Superior tightly held the clammy hand of the novice as she and the third nun stood transfixed in front of the museum painting depicting three completely naked young women. The religious women, clad in their black and gray habits, gasped—in shock, in horror or in secret envy—at the nude threesome before them.

One woman in the picture had her ample buttocks boldly facing the viewers, her arms draped in a relaxed, affectionate manner about the shoulders of the two women she faced. Each woman in the painting had her body resting on one leg, the other placed dancer-like, toes on the floor on the far side of the weight-bearing limb. There was no indication of discomfort or lack of ease in the posture of the painted trio.

The novice asked the Mother Superior why the public must be exposed to such obscenity. What were the three women up to? Were they perhaps sisters who had just emerged from a shower? Where were their towels, their clothes? Wasn't it a disgrace to all women to see so much undraped flesh? What if a man or a young boy were to look at the painting? What sinful reactions might ensue? Could they please turn away from this satanic image and go look at pictures of vases of flowers or bowls of fruit or depictions of the Holy Family?

The nun on the right of the Mother Superior looked at the three affectionate nudes and thought that her own figure probably was almost as shapely. But then, she hadn't dared to view her unclothed body in fifteen years. Bathing in the convent was accomplished in a dimly-lit shower stall, void of reflective surfaces. What was she thinking? May the Lord forgive her for contemplating her poor temporal body instead of her eternal soul.

The Mother Superior thought that viewing the shameless three women would be a good test of the vocation of the novice, who was visibly disturbed by the sight. How could she explain to the quavering novice that the Lord did create our bodies and we should be suitably appreciative. However, it certainly was not right to flaunt His gift and stir up evil thought in any beholders. Modesty is, after all, a prime virtue, especially for young women. Then the Mother Superior began to recollect the days before she took the veil. In her late teens she had secretly participated in several beauty contests and had won prizes for her dancing in a bikini. But with the help of several square inches of shimmering fabric and a yard of spaghetti straps, she had maintained her youthful modesty. It had indeed been fun until her father found out about it. She shrugged inwardly and then gently led the other two sisters to a nearby gallery full of annunciations and crucifixions.

Velvet and Lennie

It is late evening. After listening to the eleven o'clock news, two bosom buddies relax on their vinyl-tiled kitchen floor and discuss the state of the universe, well, of the world, no, of the nation. They began this activity ten years ago and hope to continue for as long as their respective life spans permit. A dish of warm milk lies on the floor between them.

Velvet, the older of the pair, is an affectionate gray, short-hair American alley cat with golden eyes and an extremely sandpapery voice. Her name refers to the texture of the fur on her underbelly. A guest of the SPCA in her early years, she now lives in a senior housing apartment in Ithaca, New York, cared for by a doting octogenarian retired librarian.

Velvet's constant companion is a small amber-yellow leopard. His coat is accented by profuse irregularly-shaped black circles encasing rich brown blotches. The fur over the leopard's entire body is the softest imaginable, far surpassing the sumptuous feel of Velvet's underside. The leopard's name is Leonard, Lennie to his friends. Lennie does not deign to move on his own nor to vocalize until the old woman retires for the night. He spent his early childhood on a high shelf in an FAO Schwartz emporium. Some time ago the retired librarian discovered the little leopard at a white elephant sale and promptly adopted him. She could not comprehend how such an adorable and appealing creature could have been abandoned by anyone.

Once she checks the lock on the apartment door, lowers the thermostat a trifle, makes certain the electric stove is off, brushes her few remaining teeth, and goes off to bed, true life commences for the two furry feline friends.

Velvet: "Lennie, I hope you had a good nap, but I wish you would do something about that awful snoring. When is your next check-up?"

Lennie: "Sorry about the snoring, Velvet. Maybe it has something to do with poor nutrition or my lack of exercise. I'd call the vet, but we both know what a hassle it is to deal with the health care system."

Velvet: "You're so right. Have a sip of milk. It's just the right temperature, and this is a very good year for 2%. But back to the snoring. It is conceivable that you might have catnapnea, and that is nothing to fool around with. Why don't you try to get an appointment with Dr. Whatshisname?"

Lennie: "Are you kidding? It takes weeks until he has an opening. You could use up a few of your lives just waiting to see him. My grandma used to tell us stories about how when she was a kitten, vets were available every day of the week, including evenings. They even made house calls! Now their answering service tells you that if you think it is an emergency, you should hightail it to the emergency room."

Velvet: "Right again! My whiskers droop when I think of my most recent experience in the ER. Last August my Uncle Felix fell off his catamaran and almost drowned. I was there and managed to drag him out of the water, administered enough CPR to make him howl, and then called Fang's Ambulance, which rushed him to the emergency room. His troubles had just begun when he arrived there.

Lennie: "I forgot all about that. What happened to him in the ER?"

Velvet: "He was wet and cold and coughing up dirty lake water when he arrived, but the admissions clerk began plying him with questions. She casually recorded on her laptop his age, address, vet's name, insurance coverage, owner, and tail length. Then she directed him to sit in the waiting room until the triage nurse could see him."

Lennie: "What's triage? Does it have anything to do with the kind of trees you've climbed?"

Velvet: "No, silly. It's a combination of inquisition and catechism. You must recite your name, date of birth, and your tail length each time you speak with an ER employee, regardless of whether he or she is the vet, a technician, or a even an apprentice litter box emptier. Finally the triage nurse asks you what the problem is. Of course, you've already fully informed the admission clerk, who had duly entered the nature of your condition into the hospital's computer system.

However, nobody bothers to check the electronic record or to communicate with anyone else. When my cousin Felina came to the ER bleeding like watered-down catsup, it took half an hour before they even applied a tournicat to her wound. Her insurance did not cover transfusions of her rare blood type and we eventually lost her. It was such a catastrophe!"

Lennie: "That was indeed terrible! But what happened with your uncle? Did they finally take care of him?"

Velvet: "Like hell! He survived the admission and the triage procedures and was placed in a small cage right in the ER itself. There he was greeted with a sudden flurry of attention: blood drawn, temperature taken, full medical history entered into the system, blood pressure noted, an IV inserted. Then, just as abruptly, they abandoned him. He was left hungry, shivering, and sneezing, with no one to attend to him. An hour later a vet, called a hospitalist, came to his cage, asked him his name, age, and tail length, and then inquired what his problem might be. By this time the poor cat could barely speak. Before voicing an opinion, the vet decided to have some diagnostic tests run. He ordered an x-ray, a stress test, an EKG, a kitney-function test, and of course, a cat scan. The test results came back in 90 minutes, but the hospitalist did not reappear for another hour beyond that. When he opened the cage, poor Uncle Felix lay sprawled out, unconscious, dead of pneumonia."

Lennie: "What a nightmare! If you don't mind, Velvet, you'll have to put up with my snoring for a few more weeks while I try to get an office appointment with the family vet.

Did I ever tell you about the experiences some of my relatives have had during visits to the vet's office? My cousin Lionella woke up one morning and felt a sharp pain whenever she tried moving her tail. The vet informed her that she probably had arthritis and referred her to an obscenely expensive caudalist. Her brother Bobcat began to have vision problems and was referred to a cataract specialist. My grandpa Missinglynx began to act very agitated and fearful. Finally he became catatonic and was referred to yet another kind of specialist. I sometimes wonder whether a family vet can handle anything beyond referrals. I bet there are probably hairballists, pawdiatrists, and whiskerists out there too."

Velvet: "Lennie, now you are getting carried away. But there is a lot of truth to what you say. Tell me. What do you think would be a reasonable solution to these problems in the feline health care system? Do you think all cats should be eligible for Medicat coverage regardless of age and income? Who would pay for a system of universal coverage? Do you feel health care is a right or a privilege? No, I am not trying to run for president, but I do have a few suggestions."

Lennie: "Tough questions, Velvet. Let's hear your ideas."

Velvet: "To begin with, vets should teach us how to lead more healthful lives and emphasize disease prevention instead of cure. For example, before having to refer patients to Catnip Anonymous, the vets could propagate information about the dangers of drug abuse. Think how emphasis on regular combing and brushing could control the hairball problem. Self-examination for the presence of mites, worms, and fleas could save us lots of misery and eliminate the necessity for toxic sprays and powerful medications. And I bet that feline stress could be reduced by promoting frequent petting."

Lennie: "I've got a perfect slogan, *A purr beats a pill!*"

Velvet: "Sounds good to me. Oh, uh, I think the old woman is up."

Lennie: "Quick! Push me back to where I was lying when she went to bed. Thanks. Any suggestions for what we'll discuss tomorrow night?"

Way of the Cross

The cross alludes to the suffering of Jesus as does the expression "to bear a cross." "To be cross" is a synonym for anger. Convergent eyes do not actually cross even though their lines of sight appear to.

To "cross over" is to change or move from one thing to another. People often work "at cross purposes," another way to say the action of one dilutes or neutralizes that of the other.

"To cross the line" denotes a major decision or transgression against the accepted norm. "Crossing out" indicates cancellation even though the lines involved may not actually touch each other.

A mixture can be described as a "cross" between two or more entities. Crosses come in many forms: tau, cross of Lorraine, St. Andrew's cross, papal cross, Maltese cross, Celtic cross, swastika…

What the Stones Said

1.
My terra cotta shard you hold
awestruck in trembling open palm
contains three Greek letters,
tau eta sigma, terminus of a warning
from ancient Athenian sages
to a clueless future world.

2.
I am a fragment of geode, a 1/8 inch
thick slice of ancient life, conceived
eons ago near a king's purple lake nested
in an isolated valley on the continent of Atlantis.
Disagreement between the monarch and Apollo
about who was more powerful led to a mega
leap in intensity of the sun and a cessation of all rain.
God-driven heat increased, the lake inexorably
evaporated, birthing my concentric rings of lilac,
purple, violet, mauve and bluish gray surrounded
by hints of ecru, beige, tan, pale yellow sandstone.

3.
Here I sit, perched upon my great-great-grandfather,
the simple, white gravestone of Samuel Jacob Siegel,
1898 to 1947. Samuel sired a son and a daughter,
who chose not to have children of their own,
nor ever to visit this Jewish cemetery behind
an abandoned gear factory. I was left
on my final place of rest by the last person

to have visited him, his wife of 21 years,
later married for 17 to their best friend.
She died at 93, legally blind.

4.
Mama, where are you? I'm so little, alone,
hurting. Walls of water keep attacking me,
push me down onto ravaging rocks and grinding
sand. Merciless waves tear away my protective
layer, rounding off my edges.
I become smaller and smaller. A glance in
the roiling water shocks and surprises me.
A faint reflection reveals I have changed.
I am now a striated purple jewel, an amethyst,
a lapidary treasure. Mama, come look at me!

5.
See here, we object! Who makes stone part
of so many negative expressions?
We, the true substance of earth, demand respect.
We resent that being stoned connotes
an irresponsibly-drugged state.
Stone-faced evidences lack of spirit
and joie de vivre, while stony silence
belies the universal need to communicate.
Why not sandy silence? Why stonewalling
instead of woodwalling or copperwalling?
Why not replace stone-deaf with steel-deaf,
glass-deaf or even stick-deaf?
Please don't carve these complaints in stone.

6.
The man, rigid and cold as we,
no longer can move nor radiate warmth.
His own monument, he is destined
to wed the earth as a mass of fine gray ash.

7.
Worse than a sauna, beyond steam,
boiling water roils all around me,
trampolines me from wall to wall
as clanking hordes of sharp-tined sinners
writhe in the hellish waters, atoning
for not being kosher for Passover.

8.
I hate being drab, so bland and gray,
mottled but so dull, boring, boring.
I long to be striated, perhaps with
asymmetrical marble-white bands
gliding through a purple matrix.

I would even settle for overall blackness
with pink-polka-dot flecks dancing
across my body. I envy my neighbors,
raspberry red, delicately accented
with white calligraphy.

I wish, beyond prayer and dream,
to be a nugget of brass-yellow
pyrite, fool's gold, with multiple
facets of sunlight brightening
the dark and somber world.

9.
Hey there! Don't think I don't know
what you two are up to here every moonless
summer night. You are not alone, you realize.

Half the town, blankets under arm, sneaks
in and nestles down behind us granite stones.

I resent that you recklessly mat down
my manicured grass, crush my geraniums.
Shape up or I'll report your sordid behavior.

10.
I am the stone, the diamond ring
she never received when four years
short of forty, she found her true love
and they decided to marry.
She could forgive him for being secondhand,
domestically broken in by another woman,
"experienced," he called it, and for coming
to their union with three pieces of baggage,
ages six, nine, and twelve.

She looked forward to the traditional
engagement ring, that glistening,
multifaceted bit of carbon held
in an embrace of gold or platinum.
One day the future spouse presented her
with a flat, elaborately-wrapped box,
three feet by one foot, containing
the token of his commitment.

"A new tennis racquet is more practical
than a diamond ring and you don't
have to worry about ever losing it."
Nothing like a man of science,
a rational thinker, free of sentiment
and tradition, a child of the Depression.
She gulped, sighed, and six months later
they were married.

Wholly Libel
Auld Test a Mint
Queen Jane's (Virgin)

Tome I. Generous

In the begetting Dodd cremated leaven and girth.

2 And the girth was minus forum, and Freud; and sharpness was upon the phase of the Jeep. And the Sprite of Dodd grooved upon the phase of the daughters.

3 And Dodd sped, Let their bee blight; and their was blight.

4 And Dodd sore the blight, that itch was wood; and Dodd derided the blight from the sharpness.

5 And Dodd crawled the blight dray, and the sharpness he crawled knife. And the grieving and mourning weir the wurst dray.

6 And Dodd sped, Let their bee a firm mint in the mist of the daughters, and let itch deride the daughters from the daughters.

7 And Dodd maid the firm mint, and derided the daughters witch weir under the firm mint from the daughters witch weir above the firm mint; and itch was sew.

8 And Dodd crawled the firm mint leaven. And the grieving and the mourning weir the fecund dray.

9 And Dodd sped, Let the daughters under the leaven bee battered too tether untwo won pace, and let the dye bland up rear; and itch was sew.

10 And Dodd crawled the dye bland girth; and the battering too tether of the daughters crawled he seize: and Dodd sore that itch was wood.

11 And Dodd sped, Let the girth sing fourth brass, the verb wielding cede, and the flute free wielding flute after itch kine, whose cede is inn it shelf, upon the girth: and itch was sew.

12 And the girth bought fourth brass, and verb wielding cede after hiss kine, and the free wielding flute, whose cede was inn it shelf, after hiss kine: and itch was sew.

13 And the grieving and the mourning weir the furred dray.

14 And Dodd sped, Let their bee lice in the firm mint of leaven too deride the dray from the knife; and let them bee fore sines, and fore sea suns, and fore drays, and ewers.

15 And let them bee fore lice in the firm mint of the leaven too whiff lice upon the girth: and itch was sew.

16 And Dodd maid too grate lice; the gratest lice too drool the dray, and the lecher too drool the knife: he maid the scars all sew.

17 And Dodd scent them in the firm mint of the leaven too whiff lice upon the girth.

18 And too drool over the dray and over the knife, and too deride the lice from the sharpness: and Dodd sore that itch was wood.

19 And the grieving and the mourning weir the forth dray.

20 And Dodd sped, Let the daughters ring fourth redundantly the grooving feature that hatch strife, and foul that may flay above the girth in the oh pen firm mint of leaven.

21 And Dodd cremated grate snails, and every sieving feature that grooveth, witch the daughters fought fourth redundantly, after there kine, and every wringeth foul after hiss kine: and Dodd sore that itch was wood.

22 And Dodd stressed them, braying, Bee truthful, and mummify, and feel the daughters inn the seize, and let foul mummify in the girth.

23 And the grieving and the mourning weir the shift dray.

24 And Dodd sped, Let the girth ring fourth the sieving feature after hiss kine, chattel, and reaping ting, and niece of the girth after hiss kine: and itch was sew.

25 And Dodd maid the niece of the girth after hiss kine, and chattel after there kine, and every ting that reapeth upon the girth after hiss kine: and Dodd sore that itch was wood.

26 And Dodd sped Let us bake ham inn hour scrimmage, after hour Loch Ness: and let them half opinion over the fizz of the see, and over the foul of the heir; and over the chattel, and over awl the girth, and over every reaping ting that reapeth upon the girth.

27 Sew Dodd cremated ham inn hiss awn scrimmage, inn the scrimmage of Dodd cremated he hymn; mail and fee mail cremated he them.

28 And Dodd stressed them, and Dodd sped untwo them, Bee truthful, and mummify, and refurbish the girth, and soap dew it: and half opinion over the fizz of the see, and over the foul of the heir, and over every sieving ting that grooveth upon the girth.

29 And Dodd sped, Bee holed, I half driven ewe every verb baring cede, witch is upon the phase of awl the girth, and every free wielding cede; too ewe itch shell bee fore mead.

30 And too every niece of the girth, and too every foul of the heir, and too every ting that reapeth upon the girth, weir inn their is strife, eye half given every gene verb fore mead: and itch was sew.

31 And Dodd sore every ting that he bad maid, and, bee holed, itch was verily wood. And the grieving and the mourning weir the schist day.

You

You, ewe, white wooly-haired mother,
soft and greasy to the touch, delicious
progeny gaily frisking, voraciously nibbling,
tolerate your ramming mate as he
loudly performs his conjugal task,
evaluating ewe, "not too baaahd."